Advance Praise for
Creating Your Future

"If your life is as touched by *Creating Your Future* as much as my life has been touched by the work of Dave Ellis, then you too will be forever grateful. Read this book and act on it, and you will not only be giving a gift to yourself and those closest to you, but you will also be giving a gift to the entire planet."

—Sam Daley-Harris, founder of RESULTS
and director of Microcredit Summit

"These simple, powerful exercises brought forth my creativity and helped me see myself more clearly. They are valuable for everyone."

—Steven Donovan, past president, Esalen Institute

"*Creating Your Future* outlines a process for increasing how we can bring creativity and natural genius to our day-to-day work. Dave Ellis has convinced me that visioning decades into the future is a practical way to bring excitement and energy to my work."

—Muhammad Yunus, founder, Grameen Bank

"When the words *create, future,* and *dreams* are combined in one book title, we are likely to consign it to the dust heap of wishful self-help. Think again. *Creating Your Future* is an intensely useful means of changing one's life. There is nothing magical about it; its practicality will send tremors through all your resistance points. Dave Ellis uses and teaches a proven method that will make you laugh, cry, exult, and get to work."

—Paul Hawken, founder, Smith & Hawken, and
author of *Next Economy, The Ecology of Commerce,*
and *Growing a Business*

"A clear, concise guide to making the most of your precious life. My experience corroborates the teachings of Dave Ellis. This book is a gift to the reader, and to a brighter future for the human family on planet Earth."

—Hazel Henderson, founding commissioner,
the Global Commission to Fund the United Nations,
and author of *Building a Win-Win World*

"In *Creating Your Future*, Dave Ellis gives readers the fundamentals, the insights and the tools to take complete charge of their luck and their lives. The book itself is as delightfully easy to read as the life it makes accessible to readers will be delightfully easy to lead. Rarely have I encountered wisdom served up in such easy-to-digest, bite-size chunks, and yet it is wisdom that can nourish me for a lifetime. The future is something that you can control, regardless of what you may think at this moment. This book shows you how to make the most of the moment in which you now live and in all those upcoming moments in which you will reside."

—Jay Conrad Levinson, best-selling author of *Guerrilla Marketing*

"Dave Ellis has taken the principles of success, life enhancement, and the enrichment of our soul purpose and organized them so clearly, lovingly and helpfully that once you read this book, you have no excuse for not fulfilling your dreams. I highly recommend it."

—Barbara Marx Hubbard, cofounder of Foundation for
Conscious Evolution and author of *Conscious Evolution:
Awakening the Power of Our Social Potential*

"For the first time in human history, the future has become completely open to human imagination. *Creating Your Future* challenges us all to take seriously the fact that our future can be as we imagine it if only we are willing to envision what we wish to become."

—James Garrison, president, State of the World Forum

"Dave Ellis's *Creating Your Future* teaches us to shapeshift our energy into forms that help us soar to new heights of personal achievement. A magical formula for transforming dreams into reality."

—John Perkins, author of *Shapeshifting*
and *The World Is as You Dream It*

"*Creating Your Future* does such a service that it is difficult to find words to express the gift that you are to all your readers. . . . This remarkable process that enables people to look more deeply into who they are and the legacy they will leave on this planet . . . is simply extraordinary. As an executive, as a leader, as a human being committed to making a difference with her life, *Creating Your Future* has impacted me deeply and emboldened and empowered me to go beyond what I thought were my limits. Thank you from the bottom of my heart for the contributions you have made to me personally, and congratulations on the contribution you are making to the great leaders of our time."

—Lynne Twist, coauthor of *The Soul of Business* and
*Money, Money, Money: The Search for Wealth
and the Pursuit of Happiness*

"*Creating Your Future* shows you how to create your life as opposed to living the life you were dealt. It has profoundly affected my work and has given me a whole new perspective on the possibilities for my life."

—Lynn McMullen, executive director, RESULTS

"This energizing book will transform your relationship with the future. Dave Ellis's empowering approach to long-range planning is masterful in its simplicity and clarity."

—Duane Elgin, author of *Voluntary Simplicity*
and *Awakening Earth*

Creating
Your Future

Books by Dave Ellis

Becoming a Master Student

Career Planning

Human Being

Learning Power

Creating Your Future

Life Coaching

CREATING YOUR FUTURE

Five steps to the
life of your dreams

DAVE ELLIS

Houghton Mifflin Company

BOSTON   NEW YORK   1998

The unique symbols (similar to ✳) at the beginning of each chapter and by each main article represent the kind of creation that is recommended throughout this book. Each symbol is a different random, dynamic, unpredictable element (much like the future) designed to inspire, challenge, and remind you that the future can be whatever you create it to be.

For information about permission to reproduce selections from this book, write to Permissions, Houghton Mifflin Company, 215 Park Avenue South, New York, New York 10003.

Library of Congress Cataloging-in-Publication Data

Ellis, David B.
    Creating your future : five steps to the life of your dreams / Dave Ellis.
        p.   cm.
    Includes bibliographical references.
    ISBN 0-395-90248-7
    1. Goal (Psychology).   2. Planning.   3. Success—Psychological aspects.   I. Title.
    BF505.G6E55   1998
    158.1—dc21   98-29799   CIP

Printed in the United States of America
QUM 10 9 8 7 6 5 4 3 2 1

A note about gender-fair language
In order to be gender inclusive while avoiding awkward sentence constructions, the author chose to alternate the use of male and female pronouns throughout *Creating Your Future*.

To Trisha, Snow, Berry, Sara, and Elizabeth,
who each add to my reasons for looking decades
into the future when I choose what to do
with every hour of the present

Contents

The Life of
Your Dreams

*Look forward. Turn what has been done
into a better path . . . Think about the impact of
your decision on seven generations into the future.*

—Wilma Mankiller,
the first female chief of the Cherokees

Without vision, the people perish.

—Proverbs 29:18

My purpose in writing, teaching, and consulting is to help people get more of what they want out of life. I've discovered that one of the most powerful paths to this goal is looking to the long-range future. Throughout this book, I invite you to experiment with this kind of visionary thinking and experience the dramatic difference that it makes.

My work of assisting people to create more wonderful lives began with college students, then continued with college teachers, business leaders, directors of nonprofit organizations, and other individuals. In each of these teaching situations, I saw that when people engaged in conversations about the long-range future, their lives blossomed almost magically.

In a college text that I wrote, I held out this vision to students: "You are on the edge of a universe so miraculous and full of wonder that your imagination at its most creative moments cannot encompass it. Paths are open to lead you to worlds beyond your wildest dreams."

It is with this vision in mind that I ask you: What's next? What future do you want to create? What's your dream for the rest of your life?

These are perhaps unusual questions. For most people,

creating the future is an unusual thing to do. The fact that you're using this book and setting aside hours of your life to create your future puts you in a group of people that's quite small — perhaps less than 0.01 percent of the world's population. Amazingly, most people spend more time planning their next vacation than they do planning the rest of their lives.

Creating the future means *choosing* what you want to have happen for many years to come — not merely *predicting* what you think could happen. This concept might seem a bit strange. When I ask people to set long-term goals, they often say, "What I'd like to do next summer is . . . ," or "For next month, my main objective is . . ." To such answers, I reply, "That's fine. And I'm suggesting that you also plan even further into the future — years, decades, even centuries from now."

You might wonder how any of us will ever know what's going to happen in a hundred years. We won't. We'll all be long gone by then. The idea is not to know the future by prediction, but to create the future by vision. We can think, write, speak, and dream about what we'd like to have happen, not just on the horizon but beyond it. We can each realize that our dreams for the future and our actions today can affect our grandchildren and their grand-children's grandchildren.

Creating the future worked wonders for me. A few months after starting my first major business, College Survival, Inc., my coworkers and I created a long-range vision for the company. The plan detailed where we wanted to be in twenty years. Within twelve years we accomplished most of our twenty-year goals — projects that looked completely outrageous when we initiated them. They included giving away millions of dollars, providing employees with benefits and salaries that went beyond the market standard, and directly teaching success strategies to tens of thou-sands of college teachers and millions of students. We also accomplished selling over three million copies of *Becoming a Master Student*, and it became the best-selling college textbook in the United States. Creating a detailed, long-range vision for the future helped us meet these goals.

This long-range vision worked so well in my business that I decided to try it in my personal life as well. I met with two friends, and over the course of a year we spent at least two hundred hours together creating comprehensive visions and plans for the rest of our lives. Though parts of our plans overlapped, they were mostly independent. Our creations represented what each of us wanted to accomplish for the rest of our lives—and what we wanted to see accomplished long after we were dead. We worked as a group to enhance our creativity and then to support each other in fulfilling our plans.

For me, the end result of this envisioning and planning work was a seventy-three-page, single-spaced, typewritten document that contained hundreds of goals—all prioritized and categorized. This document outlined in detail what I wanted for the future. Since then I have been shocked at how much of this dream, that seemed completely unpredictable, has actually come true. Many of my relationships were transformed. I did much of the traveling that I had envisioned. My financial independence has been well secured, and my health practices and physical fitness have improved dramatically.

When I saw the success of this kind of long-range vision in my work and in my life, I started teaching this practice to others. The results have been equally impressive. The people I worked with were amazed by how positively their lives changed when they focused on exactly the kind of future they wanted. This process also worked for organizations at local, state, national, and international levels when I helped them create their visions for the next five, ten, twenty, fifty, one hundred years and more.

Sometimes my request for long-range vision is greeted with skepticism. Recently I spoke to a community service club in my city and told them about my work to help people think fifty years and more into the future. When I said that, most of the members of the audience burst into laughter. Suddenly, I noticed that the group consisted mainly of older people, most of whom knew that they didn't have fifty years to live.

Although that may have been true for some individuals in the group, I think it's important to remember that we all have a future that we care about, including the future that will take place long after we're dead. We have friends, children, and grandchildren who will outlive us. We are involved in organizations and projects that will outlast us. And many of us care about the earth and human civilization as a whole, which we'd like to outlast us all by tens of thousands of years.

I invite you to join me in creating a future that you'd love. Experience for yourself the difference that creating your future can make. You have a lot at stake—the quality of your life between now and the time you die. You can thoughtfully choose what you want to do, have, and be during your life, or you can leave it to chance. The difference between chance and choice lies largely in your level of commitment to creating the future.

I wish you many hours of passionate creation—and a wonderful life.

CREATING THE FUTURE LEADS TO THE LIFE OF YOUR DREAMS

To achieve the life of your dreams, get clear about what you want in all areas of your life for many years to come.

If the rewards of a long-range vision seem unrealistic to you, stay with me for the next few paragraphs. You don't have to agree with me. You don't even have to believe what you read. I prefer that you not accept anything on faith that you read in this book.

Instead, I want you to *use* the ideas presented and experience for yourself the difference that creating your future makes. You don't need to approach creating your future as if it's an idea to be proved or disproved. Creating the future is a tool—nothing less, and nothing more. Tools are not right or wrong, true or false, good or bad. They're just more useful or less useful. What we believe about a tool is less important than whether it makes a difference in our lives.

When people bump up against a new idea, they sometimes go out of their way to analyze it or prove it wrong. They feel they have to defend themselves against the idea, almost as if it could lead to physical harm. They measure the new idea against their old ones. If the new idea contradicts an old one in any way, it gets pitched.

I ask you to approach this book with a different attitude. Filter everything you read through one question: How could I use this idea to create the life of my dreams?

Creating your future increases spontaneity

As I work with individuals from all walks of life as well as with organizations, I hear one main objection to this idea of creating the future: People don't want to give up their spontaneity. They don't want to lose their freedom.

Neither did I. The person who first taught me about long-range vision was a man named Larry David. When Larry encouraged me to develop a twenty-year plan for our business, I told him that I wanted the business to flow freely, and I had no idea what new market trends would emerge over twenty years. Besides, I started the business to gain more freedom in my life. I sure didn't want a plan that would constrain me.

"Planning will actually set you free," Larry said. "And the more you plan, the more spontaneous you will be." I thought he was crazy, but he continued to try to convince me.

Mostly to humor Larry, I took the time to develop a long-range, comprehensive business plan for the next twenty years. As I mentioned earlier, the results were phenomenal. I was amazed at how much freedom that planning provided us as an organization and as individuals.

Recently a Native American medicine man took a workshop I gave on creating the future. Months later, at a reunion of workshop participants, he said he was shocked to discover that freedom is possible within structure. "Before I came to this workshop," he said, "I hated structure and planning because I thought it did not allow spontaneity. But now I see that I can spontaneously step away from my projects at any time and go swimming, or go eat pizza, or go sit under a tree for the rest of the day and not feel guilty about it. I can do that because I'm structured, because I have a plan for getting things done."

My own experience is that I am much more spontaneous when I have the comfort of knowing where I am headed. I get more value from every activity I choose since I understand how that activity contributes to my overall vision. I know the times when I'm committed to being on task and the times when I can play. I no longer have to worry about or dwell on what's coming up next. Instead, I can focus more on the moment. And I know that slight deviations from my plan will be fine since I have an overall vision of the life of my dreams, and that vision guides my actions.

Creating your future makes a difference today

This entire book is an invitation for you to focus on what you want, invent ways you can accomplish your dreams, increase the amount of thoughtful time you spend creating your future—and start living it now.

Your long-term vision can change what you do this year and this month. Your dreams can give new meaning and direction to your daily actions. Having a long-term goal to save enough money for your children's college education can affect the way you handle money this week. Setting a goal to spend less time working so that you can spend more time with your family can change the way you schedule activities today.

If you already have long-term goals or a detailed vision for your life, this book is still for you. Use *Creating Your Future* to multiply the benefits you already enjoy. And please keep in mind that the strategies I describe work, with just a little modification, for schools, universities, businesses, nonprofit groups, governments, and other organizations.

Creating your future brings new energy

Creating your future is an act of artistry, much like the work of a composer, painter, designer, or writer. When you do this kind of creating, you are the "author" of your future.

This process makes a difference. When we drift with no clear idea of what we want, we can easily end up with lives that seem unfocused and unfulfilled. Creating the future offers different results. When we determine what we want and discover ways to get it, we tap into new sources of energy. We uncover a reason to get up every day and have a ball. Sometimes all it takes is asking, "What's next in my life?"

Many of the things we hear people say hint at a quality that's missing from their lives: "I'm low on energy today. . . . I've got a bad attitude. . . . I just don't have the willpower to get it done." That quality is usually called motivation. The lack of this quality is often people's reason for not getting things done or for failing to live the life of their dreams.

Maybe our understanding of motivation is a myth. Maybe the motivation that we want to come from outside ourselves does not exist. We don't have to depend on other people or events to motivate us. Instead, we can create a vision for our lives. Painting a compelling picture of our future can raise our energy level and move us into action. The problem of no motivation often dissolves when we have a clear motive—goals that inspire our passionate commitment.

Creating your future promotes reflection—not reaction

Throughout this book I invite you not only to think about the life of your dreams, but also to speak and write about it. Most of us find it easier to control our behaviors—including speaking and writing—than to control our stream of thoughts. An advantage to speaking and writing is that they slow down our thinking. Through the spoken and written word, our thinking becomes visible to us. This helps us to be more clear about what we choose.

Every day you make hundreds of choices. When you have a crystal-clear vision of the life you want, you can make those choices based on prior reflection rather than immediate reaction. You don't have to submit to the pushes and pulls of moment-to-moment circumstances. Your day-to-day choices can be rooted in previously created plans rather than fleeting impulses.

The huge number of choices about what to do with our time can be mind-boggling. Each of us has more options than we can possibly act on. There are hundreds of possible friends to make. There are dozens of possible careers that each of us could enjoy. Given an hour of free time, we can choose from thousands of books to read, hundreds of magazines to skim, and dozens of television programs to watch. Some refer to this problem as "option stress."

Clearly defined goals give you a way to sort through all the options and set priorities. Some will be in line with your purposes and values; other options will clearly be off track. With a clear vision of your future, you can often tell the difference in a matter of seconds.

Creating your future works

If you want examples of successful long-range visions, look to history. During the 1960s, President John F. Kennedy called for a landing on the moon within ten years. Lacking that vision, we might still be trying for a successful lunar expedition. The interstate highway system was conceived by President Dwight D. Eisenhower as a fifty-year project, another example of long-range vision. Martin Luther King, Jr., and other leaders of the civil rights movement knew they were not going to make the gains they wanted in five or ten years. They envisioned a sustained effort over decades. Elizabeth Cady Stanton and other feminists at the beginning of the twentieth century knew that the future they envisioned for women was a multidecade, maybe even multicentury, dream. Nelson Mandela and others committed to the end of apartheid had a vision that they were willing to give decades of their lives to achieve.

These examples demonstrate that one of the most powerful ways to get what we want in life is to look forward over many, many years. Just think about what a difference this strategy could make if it was widely applied. Elected officials could consider the impact of their policies over the long-range future instead of merely until the next election. Manufacturers could look ten, twenty, fifty, or more years into the future and find sources of long-term profits with fewer unintended consequences, such as pollution and resource depletion. We know that if we continue to destroy our environment at our present pace, the human species will end—and that will not be good for business.

Creating your future is fun

Generating goals can be both high adventure and a rollicking good time. Actually meeting those goals and watching the results unfold take the enjoyment to an even higher level.

Many people have so little experience with creating the future that they're surprised at how much fun it can be. Stereotypes about people who set goals still persist—that they're stuffy nerds who wear pocket protectors and carry briefcases everywhere.

Don't believe it. I don't even own a pocket protector. Creating the future is a ball. It's a powerful way to expand your mind with no drugs other than heavy doses of natural adrenaline.

When we learn ways to set goals and act on them, we can consistently experience more of what we truly want from life. We discover that the power to create the life of our dreams is a power we already have, only waiting to be used.

CREATING YOUR FUTURE SETS YOU FREE

Contrary to what many people believe, my repeated experience is that planning sets us free. In my own life, I experienced far more freedom after I got clear about what I wanted and chose ways to achieve my most important goals.

When people are feeling anxious, hopeless, or even suicidal, they often have no dream or vision to sustain them. One immediate path to feeling more calm, joyful, effective, and free is to create a plan.

When you create your future, you may find that your free-dom increases in the following ways.

You reveal possibilities

When you mentally step through your future in a detailed way, you can see options that are otherwise easy to miss. This is the same phenomenon that football players experience when they take some time between games to visualize new plays.

Great freedom and creativity arise when we step out of our day-to-day routine and examine new possibilities and paths to our goals. It's a lot easier to see options when we are not on the field in the middle of the game.

You set the plan

As you go through life, you are constantly exposed to other people's plans for you. Retailers have a plan for you to buy more. Employers have a plan for you to work more. Fund-raisers have a plan for you to contribute more. When you do the planning, you're free to choose what *you* want, instead of submitting to someone else's agenda. And even when other people set the goals, you can choose whether to accept them or not.

You can adjust the plan

An architect who has a detailed plan for a house can easily move a door one foot to the left on a blueprint. A contractor who has already built the wall and installed a door would find that change very inconvenient—and expensive—to make.

When planning a cross-country trip, a truck driver can look at several routes on a map and adjust her itinerary. It's easier to make that change than to turn around after driving a hundred miles out of her way.

These simple examples make a key point: When your goals are written, detailed, and comprehensive, you can easily examine them and make modifications up front. Making those adjustments after you've begun the project—when you've already invested time, money, and effort—is a lot tougher.

You can change the plan

If, for whatever reason, you determine that your plan needs more than a minor adjustment, then you're free to change the plan. Any effective plan is flexible. If the goals seem too restrictive, if the time lines are too cumbersome, if the vision has turned into an obligation, or if you simply change your mind—then it's time to change the plan. You can make alterations consciously, with full awareness of your values and your life purpose.

You can even change your plans often and preserve the advantages of creating your future. Those advantages come from choosing your direction and taking charge of your life.

You choose how to achieve the plan

Without a vision of the future, we might depend on other people for goals and for ways to achieve them. We could rely on others for hour-by-hour direction, something a lot of people are willing to give you—and they'll call it "management." But that kind of direction offers little freedom, little creativity, and little choice.

You can choose your way to achieve any goal. Just as you can choose many ways to travel to any destination, you can create countless ways to meet any goal. You're free to create many different paths to the same result.

You make choices with more ease

When you plan, you make the big choices. This in turn can

free up time and lessen internal debate when you make small choices. With a plan in place for this year, you can set clear goals for this month. And with goals for this month, you can choose what you'll do today. You're free from constant indecision about what to do next.

Creating a plan is like holding a magnet underneath a sheet of paper filled with iron filings. As you might remember from your science classes, the magnet pulls on those iron filings and lines them up in neat rows. Like the magnet, a plan "pulls" on our day-to-day choices and aligns them with our vision.

You increase the odds of success

Few architects propose a building project without a blueprint. Few entrepreneurs get venture capital without a sound business plan. And few film producers begin shooting without a script. Each of these people creates a vision of the future. The rationale for creating this vision is to avoid wasting precious time, money, effort, and talent.

It's amazing that so many people have no vision for something as vital as their own lives and then end up living lives of quiet desperation. Creating your future is a way to avoid that fate.

Planning to meet a goal doesn't ensure accomplishment, but it does boost the odds of achieving success. With clearly defined goals and carefully chosen action plans, you increase the probability that you'll get what you want.

Much of what people do at work and at home is simply "digging in"—frantic action with no real plan. "We'll probably never reach our goals," they might say. "But at least we're keeping busy, and we can always hope for the best." Creating your future frees you from this busywork. With a comprehensive vision for your life, you can weed out the tasks that contribute little to your goals. You can discover actions that produce results.

Writing down what you want exponentially increases your chances of getting it. When you clearly define a goal, your mind and body start to operate more consistently with your dreams.

CREATE YOUR FUTURE—NOW

Experience the subject of this book in a direct way. Start creating your future—right now, right off the bat, without further delay.

Keep a visible record of your insights, reflections, dreams, goals, and intended actions. There are many ways to do this. One low-cost, flexible, and practical method is to get lots of 3 × 5 cards. I like to write on 3 × 5 cards so that I can easily generate, sort, eliminate, and store ideas. You could also write on Post-it notes, in a bound journal, or on a computer. The important thing is to consistently keep a written record of the life that you want—a record that you can access any time.

The following is one goal-setting process you might find useful. I suggest that you read the instructions, experiment with the process, and then start writing.

1. *Write a lot.* Just write down anything you want to have, do, or be in the future. Describe any change you'd like to make— any new outcome in your family life, social life, health, career, or other aspect of your life.
2. *Write a lot more.* Brainstorm as many goals for your life as you can. Do this for at least five minutes. As you write, keep these suggestions in mind:
   * If you're using 3 × 5 cards, write each goal on a separate card. Write in the middle of the card and orient the card vertically. Later I will suggest that you write something in each corner of the card.

* Work quickly. Don't stop to edit or criticize what you write.
* Go for quantity, not quality. If no goal comes to mind right away, just write down something—*anything* you'd like to see happen in the future.
* Don't worry about *how* to accomplish any of these goals. You can create specific action plans later.
* Don't throw away a goal if it sounds silly or unrealistic. The time to revise, scale back, or toss goals out will come later. For now, give your creativity free rein. Consider even the most outrageous possibilities.

3. *When you've written goals for at least five minutes and feel that it's time to stop, take a break.* Breathe deeply and congratulate yourself. These few minutes could be the first step on a path that dramatically alters your life.

4. *Save the goals you've written and store them in a safe place.* Later I'll suggest many ways to review, edit, and organize these goals. They contain the seeds of your future. Treat your creations with care.

Those are the instructions. Now, please, write.

SAMPLE GOALS

The following is a random list of goals written by people who have taken the *Creating Your Future* workshops that I lead. Read through this list to stimulate your imagination. Perhaps you'll see a goal you'd like to make your own. Great! Steal freely. Write down any goal you like. Or take a goal and rewrite it to fit *your* personal vision for the future.

Be a skilled listener.
Travel to India.
Start a consulting business.
Visit all the hot springs in the world.
Learn to play the piano.
Own a ranch in a beautiful valley.
Be more loving.
Be more physically fit.
Be funnier.
Help create an environment that will sustain life for
the next five thousand years.
Clean out my garage.
Clean out my neighbor's garage.
Stop at the store to pick up orange juice on my way
home from work.
Eat a cheeseburger with coffee sometime before I die.
Build a YMCA on every Indian reservation.
Build a state-of-the-art recording studio, and open it to
thousands of people for free.
Establish a foundation to give soccer scholarships to
poor children.
Have a gourmet cook prepare my evening meals.
Pay for all my children's and grandchildren's education.
Give scholarships to women entering graduate school.
Grant money to people who start businesses that provide
environmental or humanitarian benefits.
Have more toys.
Travel for a year throughout Africa.
Write full-time.
Paint full-time.
Work only six months each year.

Move to Bali and start a renewal center for social activists.
Sail around the world.
Start a buffalo ranch.
Breathe more deeply and slowly.
Start a revolving loan program for small business owners.
Create an institute for responsible fathering.
Create cars that produce no pollution.
Eliminate barriers to worldwide trade.
Ensure that every child born has or will find loving parents.
Relate to my spouse based on his potential for the future—
   not his actions in the past.
Eradicate diabetes.
Fund shelters for the homeless in each major city
   in the country.
Buy a small country and turn it into a model for
   participatory government.
Build clinics devoted to merging alternative and
   mainstream health care.
Create a foundation to help reduce the national debt.
Get a black belt in jujitsu.
Stay calm and centered.
Review my goals weekly.
Build virtual reality simulators for training people
   to learn almost any skill—from climbing mountains
   to practicing safer sex.
Get a horse.
Pay off my credit card debt.
Spend more time playing with my kids.
Buy a new car.
Be clearly in touch with what's possible for me
   in every moment.

Have fewer and higher-quality friendships.
Be able to speak fluently about 100-, 500-, 1,000-,
*   and even 10,000-year goals.*
Be financially solvent for the next forty-five years,
*   without working.*
Restore the integrity of the ozone layer.
Eliminate racism through international law.
Cut my hair short and dye it black.
Recycle 80 percent of the world's waste.

TOOLS OF THE TRADE

As you read this book, doing the exercises and traveling via your imagination into the future, gather useful supplies for the trip. Some tools include:

* Pencils (An advantage of pencils over pens is an amazing piece of technology called the eraser. With a single stroke of this tool, you can clean the slate, rewrite your dreams, and re-shape your vision.)
* Lots of 3×5 cards—about twenty packs, or two thousand cards, just for starters
* A 3×5 card file box and at least five sets of dividers for sorting cards into categories and subcategories
* Large sheets of paper
* Felt-tip pens of several colors

I recommend that you write on 3×5 cards—one idea or intended action per card. You may be used to recording goals and to-do lists on notebook paper. Please consider writing them on 3×5 cards instead. Cards can be easily carried, stored, thrown out, sorted into categories, and then re-sorted.

A powerful but expensive alternative to 3×5 cards is a computer. Using a word-processing program, you can easily record, store, and search through your goals without fumbling through stacks of paper. With an outlining or database program, you can further edit, review, and reorganize your ideas.

Cards and computers are not your only options in creating the future. You can paint, draw, or use clay sculptures to create vivid images of what you want. Speak into a tape recorder, write songs, sing, dance—do whatever it takes to breathe life into your vision.

GETTING THE MOST FROM THIS BOOK

The author of your future is you. Your thinking, choosing, writing, speaking, and acting will determine how much success you enjoy with *Creating Your Future*—and with your life. Use the following suggestions to greatly increase the value you get from this book.

Reflect and act to unlock your dreams

Getting what you want is not rocket science. To create value from this book, you can start by doing just two things: reflecting and acting.

First, be thoughtful about what you want. Reflect on it. Define it. Write about it. Speak about it. Draw a picture of it. Paint it or sculpt it. Write a poem about it or sing a song about it. Think about the new things you'll see, hear, feel, taste, and smell when you're living the life you desire. Do whatever else it takes to create a detailed vision of the future. All these are ways of getting clear about what you want, and clarity creates a path for fulfillment.

Second, as you gain clarity, align your actions with your

vision. Getting what you want calls for *doing* something. Detailed goals and carefully defined plans are amazing creations, but they are not sufficient. Getting what you want usually means acting on those plans as well. When you move into action, your dreams start moving from concept to reality.

Creating your future involves a continuous cycle of reflection and action. By taking action, you find out which aspects of your vision, goals, and plans are workable and which can be refined. That leads to further reflection, which in turn leads to even more focused and powerful action.

Use words that move you

As you read and use the ideas in this book, please don't get hooked into one single word to describe the process of creating your future. You can use a variety of words for what you invent: *goals, wishes, dreams, visions, ideas, missions, purposes, plans, designs,* or *commitments.* Or refer to your collection of goals as a *blueprint* or a *design* for your future. Aim at creating a compelling future that inspires you to get up in the morning and play your life out fully.

Dig down into your deeper knowledge

Several models of the human mind hold that our knowledge exists in layers. One is our conscious knowing—what we know that we know. Other possible levels of knowing include our subconscious mind, our unconscious mind, our intuition, and our instincts.

Perhaps you and I share an even deeper level of knowing. We might be able to tap into a collective wisdom that goes beyond our central nervous system and allows us to know that which is universal.

Through writing down possible goals, you can discover passions, dreams, and visions that lie below the level of conscious knowing. One path to these deeper levels is quantity. Artists know this. They do hundreds of sketches before painting (and repainting) a given canvas. Novelists fill hundreds of pages, even though only a fraction of them survive to the final draft. Photographers expose roll after roll of film and then print only a handful of negatives. Through producing excess at first—and not worrying about how good it is—these people access creative reserves that lie at levels below the conscious mind. Later they sort out their work, choosing only the best efforts to complete and polish. You can follow their example. That's one reason for my repeated requests that you write many goals.

Another path to deeper levels of knowing is "crazy creation." This kind of creation occurs when we release judgments and brainstorm freely, allowing our most outlandish imaginings to surface. Throughout this book, I suggest lots of crazy creation.

We use only a fraction of our brain's potential—some say as little as 10 percent. But by freely using our imagination, we can discover the brilliance that lies within us. Test this idea for yourself, and see what happens. Act as if generating many outlandish ideas could help you tap vast new reserves—hidden layers of insights and intentions that could make a tremendous difference in creating your future.

Do the exercises

In addition to asking you to write, I will suggest other activities throughout the following chapters. These exercises are designed to help you create your future. Completing them boosts the odds that you will get the most from this book.

Your active involvement with this book is what makes it work.

You're far more likely to remember and benefit from ideas if you use them. I recommend that you do each of the exercises as you read them. I realize this may not be your preference. You might want to read the entire text without doing any of the exercises, knowing that on some level your mind is absorbing and applying the ideas. Or you might want to read large portions of the book and then return to do the exercises, which have all been marked by gray rules in the left margins.

Be willing to change

Creating the future is a process that opens up many options. Think of it as a continual unfolding. Your vision of the future can change yearly, monthly, weekly, or even hourly. At any point, you're free to reword, rearrange, reduce, or expand your original list of goals. You can even wipe the slate clean and begin the whole process again. Let your goals change as your thoughts, feelings, and circumstances change. Your vision of the future can make way for any new development in your life.

Another way to create value from this book is to let my ideas move you. Allow for the possibility that working with this book could totally alter your life. It is not the words on these pages, but what you do after reading them, that can make a difference.

Perhaps few of the ideas in this book are new to you. Using the book can still be worthwhile. Often people *know*, but don't *do*. They stockpile ideas without putting them into practice. Use this book to remind yourself of what you already know, and then move into action.

Be candid

Tell the truth about what you want in life and what you're willing to do to get it. Being candid releases the energy that's bound up in hiding the truth from others and ourselves. Once we speak openly about what works and doesn't work in our lives, we can create new options. You'll find that you get the most from this book when you practice constant truth-telling.

Be prepared for criticism

Some of your friends may look at this book and think you're strange for reading it. They might roll their eyes, grin, chuckle, or even laugh out loud if you talk about hundred-year goals. Or they might resent you for thinking that you could actually create the life of your dreams. Don't let these people stop you. Just keep creating the future and savoring the results in your own life. While you're at it, invite the skeptics to join you for the ride.

Push past limits

Be willing to take the lid off your dreams and live up to your potential. If a goal comes to mind during the fire of creation that seems too wild or wonderful for you to ever meet—write it down. Be willing to put any idea on the table. You can always edit goals later in a cooler, calmer state of mind. For now, don't place any upper limit on your ecstasy.

If you do feel discomfort, keep creating goals anyway. Use discomfort as a signal to continue creating your future, not to stop. Stay with the process. Accept any feelings of resistance. Keep thinking, writing, speaking, inventing, and dreaming. You will be rewarded.

Take responsibility

One way to get little or nothing from any book you read is to find fault with its content or criticize the author's style quickly. An alternative is to lower your expectations of the book and raise your expectations of yourself. Instead of sitting back and waiting to see what you "get" from this book, become active. Choose up front what results you want to gain from *Creating Your Future*. Also choose what you're willing to do to get those results. In this sense, the book is your creation even more than mine.

Create your future again and again

To get the most from this book, read it and do the exercises more than once. Return to this book every decade or every year. The future that you create might look very different each time. That's great. The benefit is that you stay in constant contact with the life of your dreams and your means to achieve it. With each reading, take time to dive into the process and play full out.

Create the future with others

One way to create a future that's worthy of your genius is to share this activity with people you care about. Ask friends and family members to read this book and do the exercises with you. Compare ideas. Teach the book to each other. Listen to your own and others' speaking with the idea of unleashing your full potential. One of the most loving things we can do for others is to hold their vision of the future as a sacred creation.

Be detail-oriented

You can emerge from this book with a vivid and dynamic picture of the rest of your life. That picture can be sharply focused, complete with hundreds of details about what you want to have, do, and be for years into the future.

Many people have a vague, hazy picture of their future, or none at all. Ask most people about their plans for the next ten or twenty years. You'll probably hear answers like these: "Gosh, I have no idea." "No one's ever asked me that before." "I guess I'll just wait and see what happens." "I'd like a better job." "I want to retire early." "More money would be nice." "Happy kids is what I want."

These answers are great starting points. Without more detail, though, they leave the future largely to chance.

Compare the following two answers to the question *What do you want?*

> *Well, I sure don't want to keep doing what I'm doing right now. I'm really ready for something different.*
>
> *I want to work at my current job for another three and a half years. After that, I'll have enough saved to take six months off and travel throughout Mexico. Then I plan to return home, get a degree in education, and start a new career as a Spanish teacher.*

The second statement provides a vision of the future with key details included. This statement contains a firm basis for action.

Fundraisers know about the power of details. Today there are thousands of foundations willing to give away millions of dollars to people with projects that contribute to society. The foundations want details about those projects: goals, tasks, time lines, budgets, personnel, and more. Money flows to people who know *in detail* how they'll spend it.

Business people also know the power of details. When they have a clear picture of a future business, they can raise money through banks and investors. Before parting with money, banks and investors want specifics.

There's power in detail. When your destination is clear, you're more likely to arrive there. When your goals are loaded with specifics, you're more likely to know when you've met them. That's a key premise of this book.

You don't have to agree with this idea, by the way. Just be

willing to test it for yourself. If you want to bring vision to your life, then bring life to your vision. Be willing to add the details.

Release regret and start anew

As they look back over their past, some people feel sadness and regret. Perhaps their dreams still elude them. Maybe they're still waiting for the passionate, loving partner they were sure they'd have by now. Perhaps they set other goals and missed them by a mile. Or maybe they had a vision of their future and just forgot about it. They might conclude that creating the future is wishful thinking and a waste of time.

Please don't treat yourself this way. To get the most from this book, be gentle with yourself. Forgive yourself for mistakes. Hanging on to anger, sorrow, or resentment can stop you in your tracks.

Missing a goal does not mean that you have to abandon it forever. You always have the option to draw a new lesson from your experience, create new ways to overcome obstacles, recapture your vision, and reclaim your future.

Be fulfilled, then set goals

Many people believe that you need to achieve goals before you can be happy. Their logic goes like this: Right now, you are incomplete. You're not as healthy as you'd like to be. You don't have enough money or love in your life. But if you set and achieve goals, you'll supply what's missing. Then you'll be happy. Well, that's just one point of view; consider another.

Perhaps the notion that happiness is realized only through accomplishing goals is a myth. Perhaps you can be happy *before* you set goals. Maybe the more satisfied and happy you are in the present, the more likely you are to get what you want in the future. I've written *Creating Your Future* for people who are already well-adjusted. This is not a "get well" book. It's for people without major problems—and even for people with a great life who know that life can get even greater.

I am suggesting that you create the future of your dreams while being happy—while celebrating. Right now, there is much about your life to celebrate. You have the courage to experiment with your life. You're inquisitive, willing to take risks, and self-aware. You already possess everything you need to create a wonderful life.

When I assist people in creating their future, I assume that they are already brilliant, effective, loving, wise, and compassionate. I hold each person I meet to be a genius. That's also how I see you. My task is not to supply you with something you're missing. Instead, my mission is to unleash what already exists in you, to unlock the potential you already have. By creating your future, you remove something that puts a lid on that potential—lack of clarity about what you want and how you intend to get it.

If you are not convinced and still believe that happiness depends on reaching certain goals, no problem. In the following pages you'll find hundreds of ideas about setting and achieving goals. Please discover what works for you and then use it.

CREATE YOUR FUTURE—NOW—AGAIN

Now grant yourself the gift of even more goals. Gather a stack of blank 3×5 cards or other materials for recording your goals, your dreams, and your visions. This time, give the exercise some new twists. Experiment with the ideas listed below:

* *Extend the time for your goal-setting sessions.* Start with five minutes. Then repeat this exercise several times over the next

few days and increase the time to ten, fifteen, or even twenty minutes.

* *Go beyond yourself.* Write goals for your neighborhood, city, state, or country as well as for your personal life. You might even want to write goals for the entire planet or human race.

* *Think about the long-range future.* Write goals to be accomplished in ten, twenty, fifty, or even a hundred years from now. Be willing to create goals that extend beyond your lifetime. Think about projects that others can take on when your life is over. Yes, the further out in time you go, the less likely it is that you'll live to see the goals accomplished. That's fine. Go ahead and write down the goals anyway.

* *If you're not sure what to write, just jot down a general category.* Examples are *relationships, career, money, education,* and *health.* Then write goals for that category. Writing down a category creates a space for you to change some aspect of your life. Perhaps you can't think of a goal for that area yet. That's okay. Just note the category for now and write specific goals later.

* *Do this exercise with a group of people.* People in the group can read some of their goals out loud. Ask group members to accept all the goals without criticism and to use what they hear to inspire some new goals for themselves. Creating with a group can boost your energy and increase the fun.

After you've generated goals, take a moment to reflect on the experience. Notice how easy or hard goal-setting was for you. If you had trouble writing even one or two goals, don't worry. You're flexing a new mental muscle called "creating your future." Few of us in any age group or occupation have much experience setting long-range goals. Give yourself time to get into shape and look forward to the rewards.

Keep your future safe for posterity. Store the goals you've just created in a 3×5 card box, folder, container, leather-bound journal, computer file, or another special location. If possible, label it with your name, using your best handwriting. Add a fancy design, picture, or photograph of yourself. Do whatever it takes to make a sacred space for your goals. After all, it *is* sacred: It contains your future.

FIVE STEPS TO CREATING YOUR FUTURE

The next five chapters outline a process for creating your future:

> *Step 1:* **Commit** *to creating your future.*
> *Step 2:* **Create** *a vision of your future.*
> *Step 3:* **Construct** *a plan to fulfill your vision.*
> *Step 4:* **Carry out** *your plan.*
> *Step 5:* **Celebrate** *what you've done—**and continue** creating*
> *your future.*

While I recommend that you do these steps in this order, you might want to invent your own style of creating the future and take these steps in a different order.

If you feel overwhelmed at the prospect of doing all this, then take that feeling as a kind of self-compliment. It means that you've put a lot at stake in using this book—nothing less than your future.

At the same time, it pays to lighten up. Creating your future is not something you *have* to do. While this book describes a powerful tool, it is not a panacea. There are many happy and effective people who are not skilled at creating the future.

For now, just experiment with the process. Play with it. See if creating your future has a positive impact. If it does, great. If not, leave this tool on the shelf for now and come back to it later. And as you choose, remember that creating your future can be fulfilling and fun.

My work, my intention, and my hope is to speak and write in a way that moves you to create the life of your dreams. I claim that your life can be phenomenal. You can have what you want. You can experience as much happiness, health, love, and wealth as you could ever imagine—and more. You can have a life filled with deep intimacy, vibrant health, full celebration, and daily ecstasy. One of the most powerful paths to these results is determining what you want now and well into the future, all in rich detail.

Step 1: Commit

When you want something, all the universe conspires in helping you to achieve it.

—Paulo Coelho

There is only one success—to be able to spend your life in your own way.

—Christopher Morley

SIGN UP FOR THE BENEFITS

The purpose of this chapter is to entice you into an ongoing commitment to create your future. Dreaming, goal setting, and planning are all part of this process.

You're more likely to fulfill this commitment if you buy in to the advantages of inventing your future—your life. In the previous chapter I offered you a sales pitch for creating the future, complete with a list of benefits. Now I ask that you move from reflecting on those benefits to an act of commitment.

The very act of commitment calls forth support. Once you openly declare your intention to create your future, you may find that resources for meeting your goals start to fall in place almost magically: "Hey, I know a foundation that grants money to people for the kind of projects you're describing." "You're changing careers? My brother-in-law might have some contacts for you." "You're self-publishing a book? I just met someone who's done that several times; give her a call."

Perhaps the adage is true: Once you commit to something with your whole heart, the universe moves in the direction you choose.

RELIVE SUCCESS

Describe in writing a time when you created your future and were pleased with the process and results.

To do this, recall an important goal that you set and met. This can be any goal, large or small. Examples range from starting a new career to starting a new habit, from getting a degree to getting a new stereo system.

Describe this event. Remember all the details of that experience—sights, sounds, smells, feelings, and tastes. Write about how this success felt to you. Also describe the strategies you used to achieve what you planned.

Right now, describe in writing how you could use some of those successful strategies to meet one or more of your present goals.

Later, as you tackle one of your current projects, re-create the feelings of success that accompanied the goal you met in the past.

CHOOSE YOUR RESULTS

The benefits of creating your future are linked directly to your own commitment and action. Right now, choose how your life will change after reading this book. Ask yourself: How will I *be* different after reading this book and doing the exercises? What will I *do* differently? What will I *have* that I don't have now?

These are some possible answers:

I will use these strategies to make significant life changes easily and joyfully.

*I will enjoy remarkable changes in my life and continue to use
the strategies in this book for a lifetime.
After reading this book I will transform the quality of my
life—dramatically—in just a few months.
I will use the ideas in this book to make moment-by-moment
choices that are aligned with my values and purpose.*

Write at least three goals about your preferred results. Also share these goals with some key people in your life. This increases the likelihood that you will fulfill your goals and get what you want.

DECLARE YOUR COMMITMENT

Now be more specific about how you will use this book to produce the results you have chosen. Declare your level of commitment to creating your future.

Read the following list of statements, and choose one that best describes how you will use this book:

1. I've bought the book. What more do you want?
2. I will skim the book and consider using a suggestion or two.
3. I will read most of the book and apply some of its suggestions to my life.
4. I will read most of the book and apply many of its suggestions to my life.
5. I will read the entire book and do a majority of the exercises.
6. I will read the entire book and do all of the exercises.
7. I will read the entire book, do all the exercises, and constantly search for ways to use its suggestions.

8. I will read the entire book and do all the exercises more than once, each time searching for new ways to use the ideas.

9. I will read this book and do all of the exercises many times, as if the quality of my life depended on it.

10. I will read this book and do all of the exercises many times, as if the quality of my life depended on it. And when I find an idea or an exercise that I don't find valuable, I will rewrite that part of the book so that I can use it to create the life of my dreams.

You can go even further. Be specific about the dates, times, and places where you will create your future. For instance, you could spend ten minutes at the beginning of each day to set goals. You could also spend an hour on Sundays setting goals for the week, month, and year to come. In addition, you could schedule personal "retreats"—hours or even whole days where you write about your purpose in life, basic values, and long-range goals.

You can start to enjoy the benefits of commitment right now. I recommend that you pick one of the ten statements above to express your level of commitment. Or write such a statement in your own words. Please do this now.

To get even more from this exercise, share your statement of commitment with at least one person. Let others know about your choice to create your future.

MANAGE YOUR CONVERSATION SPACE

You can reshape your relationships, your work, and the rest of your life when you alter your conversation space and move more of your consciousness into the future.

Conversation space is a new term. As I use it here, the word *conversation* includes any occurrence of thinking, speaking, writing, listening, watching, or reading. Talking with another person face-to-face is only one type of conversation. Watching television is also a kind of conversation, even if it is one-sided. Other examples of conversation include reading the newspaper, writing a letter, listening to the radio, going to a meeting, daydreaming, watching a sunset, or writing in a personal journal.

All these activities involve exposure to information and ideas and your reactions to them. These activities take up a lot of "space" in your life. That is, they make up a lot of what you do.

Moment by moment, you choose ways to fill your conversation space. Minute by minute, you make choices about where to place your attention. Every second presents you with an opportunity to choose your conversations—what you listen to, talk about, watch, and read, and think about.

Focusing on the past

Many people fill almost their entire conversation space with the past. They talk about what happened at work or school, about what they did yesterday or the day before. They focus on events that took place minutes, weeks, years, or even decades ago. The same can be said of our media. Most television programs, radio shows, newspapers, and magazines dwell on events of the past.

Focusing on the present

There is a second way that we can occupy our conversation space—focusing on the present. This is the domain of artistry, excellence, and joy. This is the focus of the tennis player at the moment of a great swing, the musician giving a great performance, the mountain climber ascending a sheer cliff. Deep friendship, intimate romance, good meals, enjoyable massage, and great sex occur when we savor the present moment.

Focusing on the future

Another option is to fill our conversation space with the future. This is the time we spend thinking, writing, reading, listening, and speaking about what's yet to come in our lives.

For many of us, conversations about the future usually focus on prediction or worry. Even in future-oriented think tanks, conversations typically dwell on forecasting or predicting. Talk seldom focuses on the future that people want. It usually concerns the future that will emerge *if present trends continue*.

Achieving balance by creating the future

Of course, conversations about the past can be wonderful, affirming, and powerful. And conversations about the present help us relax, celebrate, learn, and deepen our relationships.

There's also no problem with predicting the future in certain circumstances. Prediction is appropriate and even necessary for survival. Say that you're crossing a busy intersection on foot. You see a car running a red light and heading straight for you. In less than a second you mentally predict that you're about to be hit. You take evasive action. Prediction just saved a life.

I suggest that you commit yourself to paying attention to when your conversation space lacks balance. This can happen in many ways.

For example, people who talk and think mainly about the past often repeat the same actions over and over again in the future. Their habitual actions often mean that their circumstances in life remain fairly constant. These people could have the same job, the same friends, the same house, and the same problems—the very same problems—for many years. By focusing on the past, they tend to re-create the past instead of creating the future.

Although focusing on the present is wonderful, too much of this also prevents us from creating the future. When the present dominates our conversation space, we can drift from day to day without a vision. Instead of shaping our circumstances and creating the future, we could find ourselves passively reacting to random events in our lives.

Likewise, focusing too many of our conversations on the future could keep us from learning from the past or enjoying the present moment. At times too much of my conversation space has been located in the future. As a person who writes about and teaches about the future, I sometimes get carried away. I find myself writing so many 3×5 cards about what I want next that I forget to enjoy what I have already created.

Also, when worry and prediction dominate our conversations about the future, we find little space for creating a future that we want. Worrying about the future can become a kind of addiction that chokes off other possibilities.

We can use the following diagrams to represent these types of imbalance in our conversation space:

PAST	Present	Future

Past	PRESENT	Future

Past	Present	FUTURE

You can balance your conversations about the past, present, and future. And when you spend time in conversation about the future, you can devote most of it to creation. Instead of worrying about the future or predicting the future based on current trends, start changing the trends. Write, speak, and think about the future you want, the future you choose to have.

The next diagram illustrates a balanced conversation space, devoting approximately equal time to the past, present, and future. Note that the future is dominated by creation.

It's not useful to limit your conversations to a single period of time, just as it's not useful to eat only one food. Creating the future allows you to become trilingual—equally skilled at speaking about the past, the present, and what's yet to come in your life.

PAST	PRESENT	Worry
		Creating the FUTURE
		Prediction

NOTICE HOW YOU FILL
YOUR CONVERSATION SPACE

During the next twenty-four hours, observe how you fill your conversation space. Gain some clarity and awareness about the focus of your speaking, writing, listening, reading, and thinking. At any given moment, check to see where your conversation rests: in the past, present, or future. If you're dwelling in the future, also notice whether your focus is on worry, prediction, or creating the life you want. You can do the same while observing the conversations of other people.

To help this process work, avoid self-judgment. If your conversations are dominated by the past, simply notice this fact. Regret or self-reproach might keep your conversation about the past more firmly in place. Judging yourself only drains you of energy that could be used to heighten self-awareness and produce personal change.

At the end of this twenty-four-hour period, write about the

ways you typically fill your conversation space. Draw a diagram like the one on page 41 that depicts how much time you currently devote to the past, present, and future. Also note how much of your conversation about the future is devoted to worry, prediction, and creation.

SET A GOAL FOR YOUR CONVERSATION SPACE

One way to balance your conversation space is to devote approximately equal time to the past, present, and future—about 33 percent for each. This is only one option. You might want to devote 50 percent of your conversations to the present or only 10 percent of conversations to the past. Many other combinations are possible.

Describe in writing and with a picture the kind of balance *you* want. Also consider how you can fill conversations about the future with creative goal setting instead of worry or prediction.

FOCUS ON THE FUTURE

For most of us, balancing our conversation space means making a concerted effort to dwell more in the mode of creating the future. To do this, we can use each of the following strategies.

Change the focus

Being with someone who continually dwells on the past—his childhood, his old jobs, his old relationships, his achievements, his resentments—can be difficult. We might find ourselves thinking, "I've heard everything this person is about to say." Changing the focus of those conversations can fill the relationship with new energy and be a lot of fun.

This leads to a possible goal: "When I am with people, I will assist them in speaking about and creating the future." You can meet this goal in many ways. One is to set an example. Be a model by speaking about what you want in the future—in five years, in ten years, and over an even longer period. Another strategy is to ask questions that shift the conversation into the future. "What do you want to do for fun next year?" "In the next five years, do you want to change your job?" "Where would you like to take a major trip when you retire?" You could even make a direct request: "For the last hour, we've focused mainly on the past. Can we shift gears for a while and talk about the future?"

When meeting someone, focus on the future

You can change the focus to the future when you first meet someone. Most of our introductions start with questions that focus on the past or present: "Where are you from?" "Where did you go to school?" "What do you do for a living?"

Asking such questions is just a social habit that we can change. Instead of using the past to reveal ourselves, we could just as well talk about our vision for the future.

Sharing your goals with another person offers a refreshing way to get acquainted. You could practice by speaking about dreams and goals. Instead of asking, "How have you been?" you could ask, "What are you excited about that you have planned for the next year?" You can learn just as much about people in this way as by constantly delving into their past.

The next time you meet someone new, make it your intention to dwell mainly in the future. Ask the other person about her goals and then share your vision of the future.

Speak and write about the future

Talking about the future can be easier than thinking about it. After all, most of us find it easier to control our lips than our thoughts. (Whereas lips don't have a mind of their own, the mind *does* have a mind of its own.) When you find yourself talking about the past, you can simply speak about the future instead.

Another way to balance conversation space is to write. It's almost impossible to think about the past while writing about the future. Like speaking, writing is a physical activity that's easier to control than thinking. When you write, your thoughts can trail your pen into the future.

Immerse yourself in the future

You could dwell more in the future by going overboard in speaking about it. If your conversations during the past week have centered on the past, then focus them almost exclusively on the future for the next hour or even twenty-four hours.

Creating the future can be like learning a language by immersion. With the immersion method, students practice speaking and listening to a new language exclusively for hours or days at a time. You can use the same method to learn the language of long-term, comprehensive planning.

See what happens as you dive into the process and start speaking this new language of the future. At first you might feel uncomfortable. Accept that feeling as a sign that you're learning something new and taking advantage of an exciting opportunity.

Handle distractions

If you find yourself distracted from creating the future, you can describe each distraction on a separate 3×5 card. Perhaps you're filled with regret about a mistake you made. Describe that mistake on a card. Maybe you're worried about an upcoming task. Write that task down. You can use cards to summarize any conversation you're having with yourself in any given moment.

Now, depending on the particular distraction, you have several options for what to do with the card:

* You might file the card away. You can choose to handle this matter later. Say to yourself, "I promise to take care of this by Wednesday." You can even schedule a specific time for the task on Wednesday.
* You could destroy the card. This works well with thoughts you don't want—worries, regrets, resentments, and so on. Feel yourself getting lighter as you discard these pesky cards. To add a little drama, tear up the card or set it on fire. Let your concerns float away.
* You might flip the card over and write an action plan. Describe, step by step, how you will handle the distraction or complete the unfinished task.
* You could report your distraction. Read your card to someone else. If you're embarrassed about what you wrote, accept the feeling and report the distraction anyway. See if your distraction goes away when you report it.

With these options, you can change distractions from a pesky nuisance into a friendly reminder to focus your attention.

Ask for help

Changing the way you fill your conversation space to dwell more in the future is not something you have to do alone. You can enlist the help of others. Ask them to point out when you're speaking about the past, dwelling too much in the present, or losing yourself in worry or prediction about the future.

Your friends might appreciate this practice of shifting the conversation to the future. They might even seek you out as someone who restores balance and perspective.

START A SUPPORT GROUP

Make an agreement with several of your friends, family members, or coworkers to spend more time conversing about the future. During certain time periods—such as one day per week or one hour per day—you could even choose to talk only about the future.

If this option appeals to you, then right now, write the names of the people you'd like to involve and the steps you'll take to get their support.

GET PAST BARRIERS TO CREATIVITY

As you experiment with options for balancing your conversation space, you might find creating the future to be an intense activity. This process drives you inside yourself, leading you to speak of your innermost dreams and clarify your most deeply held values.

Creating the future takes attention, commitment, and action—and it can be a blast. While designing the rest of your life, you can be as imaginative as a composer, as expressive as a painter, and as flexible as a dancer. Creating your future is truly an act of artistry.

Creating the future is also deeply personal work that some

people find hard to do. When you bring up the subject of long-range goals, you might encounter some resistance. Perhaps you'll bump into strong social taboos against dwelling too much in the future. You might even be labeled as a "hopeless idealist" or a "pie-in-the-sky dreamer."

Here are some typical objections to the concept of creating your future, followed by a counterpoint to each objection:

"You just can't predict the future."

Some people argue that the world changes so fast that setting goals is pointless. To get past this barrier, remember that this book is not about predicting the future, but *creating* the future. In addition, goals are flexible. When conditions in the world change, you can change your goals in response.

"I can't control other people, so how can I set goals for them?"

That's right. We can't control others. We can't even control everything about ourselves. We can't totally control our thoughts, our feelings, or even some of our knee-jerk reactions.

To get past this barrier, remember that creating your future is not about controlling other people. Planning is about choosing *your* beliefs and behaviors. By clearly defining your goals and taking action to achieve them, you can usually influence people and events in a way that's consistent with your values.

When you're clear about what you want, you can also influence your internal experience. You can affect the overall direction of your thoughts. You can access more of the feelings you want to experience and even shape your spontaneous reactions to certain events.

"I set goals all the time, but I never meet them."

If this barrier comes up for you, then start with a small goal and carry it out. Choose one change in your life that you can make immediately. Then do it. Savor the resulting feeling of success. Imagine what it would feel like to experience this satisfaction more often and at deeper levels. This might be all you need to get hooked on creating the future.

Also, play with a number of strategies for meeting your goals. For example, make sure your goals are part of a vision for the rest of your life—a dream that inspires your passion and excitement. Create clearly defined goals that you freely choose, not goals forced on you by others. And promise someone you love that you'll meet your most important goals. These actions will give you that initial experience of success in creating your future.

"I can't think that far ahead."

Then think ahead as far as you can. Perhaps to you the phrase long-range future means the next five weeks, not the next five hundred years. That's fine. Just create goals with a time span that feels comfortable for now.

The key is to start exercising your planning muscles. Those muscles gain strength with steady use. The ability to set longer-range and more comprehensive goals comes with experience. Just set goals as far out in time as you can for now, then trust that you'll expand your vision with more practice.

"It's selfish to spend so much time and energy creating what I want."

It's true that creating your future is designed to raise the vitality, quality, and enjoyment of your own life. And that may not immediately change the world. But perhaps the most valuable gift you can offer the world is your ecstasy. When you're thrilled about the life you invent, you create that possibility for others.

You demonstrate that bliss is a realistic option. You model joy. You teach through the power of example — one of the most powerful ways to teach anything. When you operate from this blissful state, you're more likely to be effective, and your contributions to the world can be greater.

Your vision can also go beyond the person standing inside your own skin. Your future can include goals for your family, friends, community, city, state, and country. You can write goals for people in any country of the world. Goals for water conservation, alleviating hunger, and world economic development can all be part of your plan. This no-holds-barred approach to creating the future can include the entire globe and the six billion people who share the planet with you. That may not be so selfish.

"The methods you suggest are just not my style."

My aim in this book is simply to help you think, talk, and write more about the future you want. There are many possible ways for you to do this. Although I do recommend using 3 × 5 cards because they can be sorted, stored, and reorganized easily, there are several other great ways to represent your future:

* Draw, paint, or create sculptures to symbolize the person you'd like to be in months, years, or even decades from today.
* Write a story that describes in detail the life you would like to have in one, five, or ten years.
* Construct a three-dimensional model of a project you want to complete.
* Speak for an hour every week to someone who is committed to remembering what you want for the future.

* Meet every other week with a group of people who will remind you of your goals and support your direction in life.
* Repeat daily affirmations that plant your vision and goals firmly in your subconscious mind.
* Use a computer to capture your dreams.
* Write messages that represent your visions, using a handmade paper journal and calligraphy pens.

These are only a few options. With a willingness to experiment, you can create many more that fit your style.

"I haven't got time to set goals."

Many people know the importance of setting aside money to reap dividends for the future. They make carefully considered purchases of stocks and bonds. They spend time writing financial goals and creating strategic plans. Yet they forget to treat their future with the same care with which they treat their money.

Creating your future is an investment in yourself. It doesn't have to take much time. You could draft a life purpose statement in ten minutes. You could write a goal in one minute or less. Reviewing your weekly plan and setting priorities for the day can be done in a few minutes. You can increase the *quality* of the time you spend in conversation about the future without increasing the *quantity* of that time. Just shift at least part of your conversation from worrying about or predicting the future to creating it.

"I'm already too goal-oriented and too busy."

When presented with too many options for creating the future, some people say, "I don't want any more goals. I want to create a simpler life."

Remember that the purpose of writing many goals is not to get busier; it's to become more creative. I recommend that you write at least ten times more goals than you ever think that you will do. This allows you to choose from a big stack of wonderful options. Your resulting choice may be just three or four important goals, one of which could be to relax more.

Creating the future does not have to mean overcommitment, overscheduling, long to-do lists, and lots of added pressure. Many people set a few big goals, meet them, and stay relatively stress-free.

One of the benefits of creating the future is deciding what not to do. You can weed out low-priority activities and those that no longer create value. Filtering your choices through a few thoughtfully chosen goals can protect you from ever-increasing demands on your time. You can even set a goal to have no goals for a certain period of time, whether that be five minutes or five days.

The process of creating your future can help you purge your to-do lists and clear the clutter from your calendar. You could experience more of what you want in life by thoughtfully focusing on fewer activities of higher value.

"Once I write a goal, I feel obligated to do it."

Some people feel obligated to meet *every* goal they speak or write, and that scares them away from creating the future. Once they create a goal, they feel married to it.

You can get past this barrier by distinguishing between *possibilities* and *promises*. When brainstorming goals, you're under no obligation to meet any of them. Speaking about possibilities is a creative exercise, not a commitment to act. Promises are different. Promises *are* commitments to follow through. When you're clear about this difference, you're free to create hundreds of out-landish goals and make promises to fulfill only the ones most important to you.

EXAMINE YOUR BELIEFS
ABOUT CREATING THE FUTURE

Faced with the prospect of setting goals and creating the future we want, some of us place barriers in our way. This can take place in a split second, before we're aware of what's happening. Often these barriers are invisible and come in the form of unconscious beliefs, like these:

Change is risky and to be avoided at all costs.
Things never work out the way I want.
I don't really have what it takes to create a wonderful life.
My family or friends will resent my success.
My partner won't approve of my goals.
I want to know how to meet all my goals before I commit myself to them.
I just don't have the money or resources.

If you hold such beliefs, you might get mixed results when creating your future.

Barriers can also take the form of actions that sabotage the process of setting and meeting goals. Examples include procrastination, criticizing goals the moment you create them, and writing down only the goals you're certain you can achieve.

One way to work around these barriers is to get them out in the open and fully examine them. Once you become aware of a belief or behavior, you can accept it or change it. Sometimes awareness is enough to defuse a thought or action that deters you.

To increase this awareness, take a few minutes to list your personal beliefs about setting goals, along with any feelings associated with those beliefs. Also describe any behaviors that could undermine the process of creating your future.

Once you have written your list of beliefs, feelings, and behaviors, consider the idea that these are merely habits—things you say to yourself or things that you do over and over again. Habits can be changed. You can choose the beliefs, feelings, and behaviors that no longer serve you and replace them with new ones that help you create the future. These are examples of such new beliefs:

> *The choices I've made in the past had a big impact*
> *on my present life.*
> *The choices I make today will largely create my future.*
> *If I really want to achieve a goal, I'll make the time to do it.*
> *I've set goals in the past and met them.*
> *I deserve to have a wonderful life, and I can create that life.*
> *I can involve my family and friends in creating my future.*
> *I will shape my future, free from the constraints of the past.*
> *As I plan, I will remember and learn from the past.*

Step 2: Create

One of the saddest lines in the world is,
"Oh come now—be realistic." The best parts of this world
were not fashioned by those who were realistic.
They were fashioned by those who dared to look hard
at their wishes and gave them horses to ride.

—Richard N. Bolles

Sometimes people act as if all the possibilities for their future have already been exhausted. That's like the suggestion that was made years ago to close the patent office because there would be no more inventions.

The exercises in this chapter can keep your personal patent office open. Use them to energize your vision, give your imagination free rein, and invent hundreds of fantastic new goals. You could do all of the exercises that follow or just those that appeal to you. If you skip an exercise for now, consider coming back to it later.

As you create, keep the following suggestions in mind.

Begin with What

To unleash the master planner in you, hold off asking *how* to achieve a goal. Few commitments to great goals were ever based on preknowledge of how to accomplish them. Instead, people with big dreams often start with a vision of *what* they want and an overriding commitment to seeing their dreams come true. Often they create a goal and commit themselves to it long before they ever know how to make it a reality.

When I first decided to write and publish a book for first-year college students, I knew that I wasn't a writer and I didn't have any knowledge about publishing. I was committed to helping students and to developing a business that would enable me to work with people I loved.

Without knowing how to write a book, how to get it published, or how to sell it, I started the company. I gathered people around me who would share my commitment to write, publish, and sell a great book.

We did it. Out of this commitment and in large part because of our ignorance about *how*, we ended up writing and self-publishing the best-selling college textbook in America. Our little company actually outsold books by all of the major publishers of college textbooks. We could hardly believe it. And it all started without our knowing how.

The problem with trying to figure out how to achieve a goal before becoming committed to it is that the most effective means to a goal usually are invented in the process of achieving the goal itself. I'm glad I didn't know how to achieve my goal. If I had, I would probably have thought the project was impossible or at least far too much work. Worse yet, if I had known *how*, I would probably have produced and sold the book in the way other writers and publishers do it, and it wouldn't have worked.

Fortunately, we were naive. We had to invent a pathway to our dream, and that invention not only sold a lot of books but revolutionized one branch of college publishing. Now major publishers do much of what we did to achieve our commitment.

You can use the same plan as you create your grandest goals. In the beginning, stick with *what*, *where*, *when*, and *who*: *What* do I want? *Where* do I want to be in the future? *When* will I make my desired future occur? *Who* do I want to be with in the future?

There's nothing wrong with asking the "how question." There's a time and place for choosing strategies to fulfill goals. But in the beginning, questions of strategy can easily be overdone, leaving us focused on particular mechanics instead of the creation of a broad, rich vision of the future. Concentrating on *how* too early can even keep us from taking action: "I don't know how to meet that goal, so why even try?"

Once you're clear about *what* you want, you may find that many of the details about *how* to get it also become clear. With a detailed vision of the future, you can make moment-to-moment choices that move you closer to your goals.

Later, ask How

Once you've freely imagined *what* you want, *when* you want it, and *where* and *with whom*, then experiment with asking "how questions" to create subgoals. This means breaking a large or long-term goal into smaller steps. For example, consider the goal of getting a teaching degree. Asking "How will I get a teaching degree?" leads to subgoals such as writing for college catalogues and interviewing teachers.

A related technique is to directly restate "how questions" as goals. For example, the question "How will I slow down my frantic life and live more simply?" can become a goal: "I will slow down my frantic life and live more simply."

Then ask Why

Asking "why questions" can greatly expand your list of goals and clarify your values. Just take any goal you've already created and ask, "Why do I want to meet this goal?"

"Why questions" bring your values or "supergoals" into focus. Asking "Why do I want a teaching degree?" can lead to these answers: "To make a difference in the lives of others" and "To keep expanding my knowledge and skills." These answers reveal values of contribution and lifelong learning. Values generate and support the first goals that came to your mind. With this insight, you can write other goals to support the value of contributing to others (give away 5 percent of my income) and the value of learning (increase my vocabulary).

Conduct brainstorms

Brainstorming is a simple and powerful way to bypass the internal censors that kill new ideas. Brainstorming can help you access ideas buried in the subconscious mind—ideas that could otherwise lie dormant.

The purpose of brainstorming is to generate as many ideas as possible. Quantity, not quality, is the key. Just set a time limit and speak or write as many options as you can.

To get the most from this process, suspend judgment. List even the most seemingly impossible or impractical ideas. Later, review them with a more critical eye. Sort ideas by priority and quality. Keep ideas that you'll definitely follow up on and those that you'll consider again at a later time, and then toss out the rest.

Create many goals

Creating many goals gives you a chance to gain skill at organizing and setting priorities. That's difficult when you don't have lots of goals.

Having a 3×5 card file that's teeming with goals gives you permission to throw some goals away. This also promotes your creativity, encouraging you to create goals that at first seem silly or outrageous. With some time and thoughtful revision, these goals could turn out to be feasible activities.

Sift ideas in your subconscious mind

While creating goals, you might become confused about what you truly want, about ways to state a particular goal, or about strategies for achieving a goal. When that happens, simply take a break. After stating the problem clearly and immersing yourself in possible solutions, do something else for a while. This allows the problem to "bake" in your subconscious mind. New goals and solutions often emerge when you stop struggling with a problem or trying to force a solution.

Often a break is all that's needed for a creative breakthrough. The solution you're looking for might come while you're washing dishes, taking a walk, or changing diapers. Such unexpected discoveries are one of the pleasures of creating the future.

Do something new

"I'd never go winter camping." "Downhill skiing? That's just not for me." "I'm going to avoid that statistics course for as long as I can."

Most of us can come up with a list of things that we'd just never do. Such decisions close down possibilities.

An alternative is to pick one of those things you'd never do and go do it. This practice can recharge you, lift you out of old ruts, and grant you a new sense of your potential. In turn, these changes unleash the master creator in you and pave the way for new goals and greater joy.

Forget about time

When asked about the barriers to getting what they want in life, many people offer the same answer: "I don't have time."

Dealing with schedules is essential. But setting time restrictions too early in the planning process results in placing needless limits on creativity.

While creating goals, pretend that your time is unlimited. If this feels unrealistic, remember that you're in a creative mode for now. It's okay to think, write, or say anything. When a daring, really fascinating goal takes hold, you can often make time to achieve it. Discovering what you really want can open your eyes to resources that you've missed.

Forget about money

While you're brainstorming goals, also release any concern about money. At this stage, you can often be more creative if you stop saying, "That's a great idea, but where will I ever get the money to pay for it? I'm not rich."

Consider that, in fact, you are rich. You probably have several changes of clothing, warm shelter, a car, a television, a sound system, and enough food to prepare a variety of meals. Throughout history, most people lived without these material blessings. Millions still lack them today. Begin creating your future from a belief in abundance, not scarcity.

Also consider the possibility that money "flows" to worthy goals. Foundations and wealthy individuals have billions of dollars to give away. Most of those dollars are slated for people with a clear vision of the future and projects that contribute to society.

Another way to erase concerns about money is to discover the goals behind your desires for money. Then find ways to meet those goals while spending less money—or no money at all. Say that you want money so you can take a vacation on a secluded tropical island. Ask why you want to take a vacation. Perhaps your basic goal is to gain privacy and relaxation. Then consider ways you can get privacy and relaxation *without* traveling to a tropical island. A couple of nights in a local luxury hotel might do the trick. So might spending an afternoon in a bubble bath with a good book and the phone unplugged.

Also include financial goals as part of your vision for the future. Libraries and bookstores are full of information about taking charge of your finances. Career counselors and financial planners can also suggest money management strategies. You could start handling finances so well that money stops being a barrier to your creativity.

Turn complaints into goals

When you hear yourself complain about something, turn that complaint into a goal. For example, you might complain about the traffic on your way to work. That complaint could persist for years and get in the way of your wonderful life. Instead of just putting up with the upset, write a goal: "I want to get to work without fighting the traffic."

This goal might be accomplished in lots of ways. Each possibility can be expressed as a more fine-tuned goal: "I want to remain calm and relaxed even in rush-hour traffic." Or "I want to move closer to my job." Or "I so dislike traffic that I am going to find another job closer to my house." Or "I've always wanted to work out of my home, and now is the time to develop my own business." Or . . . let your imagination be your liberator.

It is even valuable to turn other people's complaints into goals. Let's say that people around you often complain about your being late. You could remedy this situation by choosing one of these goals: "I will be on time." Or "I am going to communicate with people so they don't expect me to be on time." Or "I am going to pretend that every meeting or appointment begins fifteen minutes before the actual time, so that I will be a few minutes early." Or . . . let your imagination be your liberator.

Turn objections into goals

Some of the goals you create might inspire objections from yourself or others. For example, someone might argue that your goal is unrealistic: "Your goal is to help invent a car that will get sixty miles to the gallon? That car won't have any power. Besides, no one would be able to afford it."

Faced with these objections, you can set new goals: "Create a fuel-efficient car that is affordable. I will make sure that the fuel-efficient car has plenty of power."

Turn self-reproach into goals

Whenever you become upset with yourself, you can turn the problem into a goal. If you discover that you are too self-conscious and often avoid saying what you really think, you don't need to hold that habit as a major personality problem. You can just create a new goal: "Be more self-expressive."

If you discover that you procrastinate too much, you don't need to hold that as a character defect. You can turn that discovery into a goal: "I will do tasks that are important to me and choose not to do the rest."

Recently I felt continually upset about being too busy and tightly scheduled. I started to dwell on what was wrong with me. That wasn't much fun. So I took this problem and turned it into a new goal that I was committed to achieve: "I will have more unscheduled time and free myself from constant awareness of the clock." When I created this goal, the problem seemed almost solved.

Of course, if I forget to follow through and move toward fulfilling my goals, then the problems and the related upset will probably continue. If that happens, I can notice that a problem in my life is persisting. And once again, I can turn that problem into a goal and create a specific action plan for achieving it.

This strategy allows you to unleash your creativity and shed a lot of problems at the same time. When you notice that something about your life is not working, you can continue to experience the difficulty or turn the problem into a goal.

Turn jealousy into goals

If you notice yourself feeling jealous, you can continue to struggle with that green-eyed monster. Or you can turn the feeling into a goal.

Recently I heard about a couple who took a two-month vacation by the ocean with their friends. I felt jealous and angry that they got to do this and I didn't. Rather than continue to live with that unpleasant feeling, I turned it into a goal: "Spend at least two weeks by the ocean with friends and family in the next six months." Though this goal may require significant planning and preparation, I know it's possible for me to achieve. And I get to turn feelings of jealousy into quality time with people I love.

Involve all your senses

You can express your goals in a variety of sense modes. If you find it hard to see the future, then think about what you want to hear, smell, taste, feel, or touch. If you're drawn toward sound, ask, "What might people be talking about in twenty years? What noise levels might exist in major urban areas? What changes are people oppressed by hunger and poverty calling for?" Or complete the following sentence: "The future that is calling me includes..."

You could also switch sense modes and imagine a time when the world is free of the stench of rivers swollen with garbage.

Listing sensory details gives new meaning to abstract goals such as reducing pollution.

Look boldly for things to change

To create new goals, open up your thinking about the aspects of your life that can be changed and that cannot. Be willing to put every area of your life on the table.

It's fascinating to notice the areas that are typically placed off limits when people set goals. Money, sex, spirituality, career, marriage, and other topics can easily fall into a category called "I'll just have to live with this."

For example, you might think that you have to live with the face you have now. Maybe not. There are ways to change your face without plastic surgery. There are dozens of muscles in the face. Learning to relax them and bring more of them under conscious control may change the way you look. Even something as simple as a smile can go a long way to changing your appearance.

When creating the future, consider the whole range of your experience. Staying open-minded can lead to a future you've never dreamed possible.

Look for what's missing in your life

Goals usually arise from our sense of what's missing in life. Goal setting is fueled by unsolved problems, relationships we want to develop, careers we still want to pursue, and projects that are incomplete. When nothing's missing, goals can seem irrelevant. Affluent people rarely set a goal to eat three meals each day.

To create the life of your dreams, release negative judgments about what's missing from your life. Forgive yourself for not attaining some of the things you want. Instead of talking about your shortcomings or deficiencies, talk about your potential. The person with a bulging belly and weak knees can honestly say, "There's a lot of potential in this body!"

Maintain what you love about your life

Not all goals need to spring from a sense of need. You can also make it a goal to maintain things that you already have or to keep doing the effective things that you already do. If you exercise vigorously three times each week, you can set a goal to keep exercising. If you already have a loving relationship with your spouse, you could set a goal to nurture that relationship for the rest of your life.

Steal someone else's goal

One way to make powerful plans is to take on other people's goals as your own. Say that you hear someone speak about creating a monument for women in Washington, D.C., by 2005. That's a goal you can steal.

This form of stealing is not illegal or even unethical. It is actually a compliment. You're signing up for the team, adding your efforts to help accomplish a goal. Many goals are more likely to be achieved when they're shared.

Create the future with others

Consider having a personal board of directors—a small group of people with whom you set goals, discuss decisions, brainstorm possibilities, and do the exercises in this book. Coach each other as you create the future.

Setting goals by yourself can expand your vision. Creating your goals with other people takes the process to a whole new level.

Be your own consultant

Step back and look at yourself as someone else might see you. Play the role of a personal consultant who sees your full potential and is committed to your success in all areas of your life. Imagine what this person would say to you, and then create goals based on what your "consultant" tells you.

Acknowledge fear

When you open up your imagination and start to create the future, you could make a discovery: The future you really want is much different from the future you've casually said you wanted in the past. That insight can trigger discomfort, fear, or denial.

When you're willing to tell the truth and put every aspect of your future on the table, almost any goal could come to mind. You might find that the life of your dreams does not include your current spouse, your current job, or your current home. The future you passionately want might include new relationships, a new career, or a move across the country.

Such discoveries can have major ramifications. Fear of those ramifications—even if you know the goals would lead to a more wonderful life—could stop you from discovering what you really want. Once you openly admit the fear, you can start to release it. That frees up energy and creativity that you can use to solve problems.

For me, one of the hardest parts of creating the future occurred when I recently started looking deeply at where I want to live. I even feared opening up the question because I had just realized a decade-long dream of building an office and retreat center near my home on 320 acres in the Black Hills of South Dakota. I spent years imagining this building. I spent months creating detailed drawings showing how every room would be designed, how every log and rock would be laid. Then for a year I devoted part of my time to overseeing the construction of this beautiful facility. With the project completed, I celebrated and then started to fear uncovering a desire to live elsewhere—and the worry that all this time and energy had been wasted.

As I'm reviewing these words right now in a spacious room in the retreat center, the jury is still out on where I'll be living in the future. But at least I've gotten past the fear of looking at what I truly want. I also realize that if I choose to live elsewhere, then this beautiful building will still be here—either for me to revisit periodically or for someone else to own and enjoy.

Allow absurdity

You might read over some of your goals and think that they look absurd: "No way. I'll never be able to do this. Who am I kidding?" Thoughts like these kill bold futures and hold people hostage to the past.

People with a grand vision are often called absurd. Gandhi was scorned when he spoke of an India free from British rule. Golda Meir spoke repeatedly of an Israel at peace with its neighbors and the entire world—a dream that still seems absurd to some. Betty Friedan was laughed at when she pioneered the feminist movement.

If your long-term goals seem outlandish, then focus on shorter-term goals instead. Look to what you can accomplish in one year, six months, or one week. Goals that are closer to the present can seem far more realistic. Just focus on meeting these goals for now. Over time, you could be shocked at how many "absurd" goals you actually meet.

TELL THE TRUTH

Telling the truth about yourself has uncanny power. Absolute honesty puts in motion a set of forces that can alter you forever. If you want to change your life, begin with the truth.

This exercise gives you an opportunity to do just that. In a few minutes from now, you will survey the whole expanse of your life. Prepare to admit your strengths and your weaknesses.

This may be the most difficult exercise in the book. It can also be the most rewarding. Doing this exercise thoroughly can take you a long way toward fulfilling your purpose in reading *Creating Your Future*.

The idea is this: Write the truth about who you are and what you want. The following instructions will guide you through the process step by step. Telling the truth is the core of each suggestion.

If you want to experience the full benefit of this exercise, then do three things:

* *Be specific.* Instead of writing, "I'm unhappy," you could write, "I feel isolated and have few people I can call on during times of crisis."
* *Be courageous.* If you start to feel uncomfortable, that's probably a clue that the exercise is working. You may be looking at parts of yourself that you'd rather not face. If this happens, acknowledge the feeling fully. Then return to telling the truth. Remember that it's difficult—if not impossible—to change those aspects of life that hide in the shadows. When you shine a light on your shortcomings, you begin to rob them of their power.
* *Be complete.* Many people think that telling the truth is a strategy that applies only to our weaknesses. This strategy is even more useful when we admit our strengths and skills as well.

As you complete this exercise, you might reveal things that you don't want others to know—perhaps things that could get you into trouble. Consider writing your responses on a separate sheet of paper and then destroying it.

Allow about thirty minutes to complete the whole exercise.

Part 1

Take ten minutes to complete the following sentences. Write at least ten responses to each one. Don't worry about the quality of what you write. Just list as many ideas as possible in the allotted time.

> *I don't feel good about myself when I . . .*
> *Things don't work well when I . . .*
> *I am ineffective when I . . .*

Part 2

Set aside another ten minutes to complete the following sentences. Again, aim for at least ten responses to each one. Don't evaluate anything that you write. If an idea pops into your head, put it down. You can review and reflect on your responses later.

> *I am good at . . .*
> *One of my strengths is . . .*
> *I am effective when I . . .*

Part 3

Now that you've finished the first two parts of this exercise, take a short breather. Also celebrate the hard and potentially rewarding work that you've done so far.

Next, take another step to solidify your insights. Review the two lists you've just created. Cross off any ideas that don't make sense. Put an asterisk next to statements that are the most accurate. When possible, reword the statements to make them more clear.

Part 4

Here's your chance follow up on what you've learned about yourself. Review your list of strengths regularly, especially when you feel discouraged or just plain stuck. You might want to rewrite this list and post it in a prominent place so that you'll see it often.

Look again at your list of problem spots from Part 1. Take the most significant items and rewrite them as goals. Move from problems to possible solutions. For example, the statement "I am ineffective when I run low on cash at the end of each month" can be transformed into this goal: "I intend to live within a budget, decrease my spending, and maintain my overall quality of life."

If any of your intentions bring up outrageous possibilities or hold the promise of far-reaching change, that's great. Consider breaking these long-range goals into simple, specific actions you can start taking immediately.

Part 5

The last step of this exercise is to go beyond writing. Take action on some of the goals. Then savor any positive new results in your life.

Come back to this exercise periodically. Use it several times to spot-check for problems and take charge of your life. You can make truth-telling a habit.

CREATE YOUR LIFELINE

Creating a lifeline is one way to discover what you want to accomplish over the entire span of your existence. You can also use this visual device to set goals that go well beyond your lifetime.

To get the most out of this exercise, be willing to let it move you. In my workshops, I've done this exercise with thousands of people. Many reported it to be a life-changing and emotional event. Some people even wept.

The following are some suggestions for making your lifeline:

1. Begin by taking a blank sheet of paper and orienting it horizontally. For ease in writing, you might want to use a large sheet, perhaps eleven by seventeen inches or larger. The size adds significance to what you're about to create.
2. Draw a horizontal line across the middle of your paper. This is your lifeline. It represents the approximate number of years you'll be alive.
3. On the far left end of the line, draw a dot and label it with your date of birth.
4. Estimate how long you might live. Then place a dot about three fourths of the way to the right, and label it with your projected date of death. Remember that this step simply serves a useful function for this exercise and has no connection to reality. You're under no obligation to die on the date you write! The purpose of projecting a death date is just to remind you that you're mortal. Do not place your date of death at the extreme right-hand edge of the line. Leave some space on the line for goals that exceed your life span.
5. Next, place a dot on your lifeline that represents the present. Label it with today's date.
6. At appropriate points to the left of today's date, plot some

significant events in your life. Examples are graduations, marriages, career changes, children's birth dates, deaths of relatives, and the dates when you landed a new job or started a business. Take at least ten minutes for this part of the exercise.

7. Now set goals for the time between today and when you might die. Do this by adding dots to the right of today's date. Label these dots with goals that represent what you'd like to be, do, or have in the future. Add a target date to meet each goal.

8. Finish your session by considering what could happen after you die. Here you can include predictable events, such as the retirement of your children or the death of a younger relative. Also think about what you want to have occur after your life is done. Include goals for your family, friends, workplace, city, community, state, country, and world. Be willing to set goals that extend far into the future.

9. Write any insights, discoveries, or lessons that emerged as you did this exercise. Then generate new goals based on what you learned.

You can repeat this exercise many times, ranging from once a month to once a decade. Each time you create a lifeline, you can gain new insights into the past and create a new vision for your future. Look at your lifeline as a living document—one that changes as you learn and grow.

At any time you can get other people into the act. For example, create your lifeline and reveal it to your partner, family, and friends. Ask them to create a lifeline for themselves. Look for points of intersection, shared events, common goals, and similar values.

Each time you do this exercise, you can allow the artist within you to emerge. Use separate colors for different categories of goals. Put your lifeline on a really long piece of paper—use continuous-form computer paper with one page representing each year of your life. Draw pictures that depict significant events—a diploma next to the date you graduated from high school, a heart next to your first date.

Your lifeline does not have to be a straight line. Experiment with circles, arcs, slopes, rainbows, or waves. If you want to invest some extra time, make it three-dimensional. Express your lifeline in sculptures, collages, paintings, or mobiles. Make that lifeline come to life.

WRITE YOUR EULOGY

Imagine that you get to attend your own funeral. (In your imagination, you can do anything, even this.) Then write your eulogy—what you'd like people to say about you on this occasion. Think about how you want to be remembered after you're gone. Please do this writing now.

Next, reflect on what you've written. Describe what you'll do to bring your daily actions more in line with your eulogy. Set any long-term or short-term goals that seem appropriate.

If you're uncomfortable with the idea of attending your own funeral, then experiment with a variation on this exercise. Imagine that you're eighty years old. Now pretend that you get to describe to your great-grandchildren the rich, satisfying life you've been able to lead. Use this description as a source of goals.

WRITE YOUR LIFE PURPOSE

The American Heritage Dictionary defines the word *purpose* as:

1. The object toward which one strives or for which something exists; an aim or goal. . . . 2. A result or an effect that is intended or desired; an intention. . . . 3. Determination; resolution.

A life purpose is the most comprehensive statement of your aim in life. An effective purpose statement is highly practical. Referring to it can tell us when our goals or behaviors are off track. With our purpose firmly in mind, we can make moment-to-moment choices with integrity.

Before you write your own purpose, keep in mind the difference between a goal and a life purpose. A goal can be fully achieved. A purpose statement refers to an overall direction in which you can travel for the rest of your life. A single life purpose can generate many goals.

Get ready to spend five minutes drafting a one-sentence statement of your purpose in life. (It can be a long sentence!) Before you write, read the following suggestions:

* To get started, prompt yourself with questions:
  What am I striving for?
  What is the aim of my life?
  What is the main result I want in my life?
  What am I determined or resolved to achieve with my life?
  Or, complete these sentences:
  In my lifetime, I want to be . . .
  In my lifetime, I want to do . . .
  In my lifetime, I want to have . . .
  The purpose of my life is to . . .

* Brainstorm several different statements of your purpose. Later you might choose to combine these versions into one statement.
* As you write, remember to focus on the purpose of your life—not of human life in general.
* After five minutes is up, spend another five to fifteen minutes revising your purpose statement.
* Finally, spend five to fifteen minutes writing goals based on your purpose. Ask yourself, "What would a person with this purpose do, have, and be during his or her lifetime?" Record your ideas.

If this task seems daunting, don't worry. You can revise your initial purpose statement later. Just pick up a pencil and write. Please begin now.

To gain more insight and generate more creative juice, do this exercise again with a group. Give people the option of reading their purpose statements aloud.

Rewrite your purpose as many times as you like. Be sure to choose words that truly move you and inspire action. A life purpose stops being useful when it no longer calls you forward—no longer inspires you. Before your statement of purpose fades or becomes invisible, revise it or create a new one.

Sample life purposes

My purpose is to live, learn, love, and laugh.

My purpose is to have a wonderful life and to dramatically contribute to the quality of life on earth.

My purpose is to develop success strategies and ways to communicate those strategies.

I intend to become financially independent and raise happy, healthy children.

I will live in harmony with all creation.

I am here in this world to give and to receive.

My purpose is to be a healing presence in the world.

My purpose is to promote the well-being of my family.

In my life I seek to release suffering and serve others.

The purpose of my life is to become an accomplished pianist.

*The purpose of my life is to live in a way that makes a
    difference for people and contributes to their happiness.*

The purpose of my life is to serve God.

The purpose of my life is to be loved and to be loving.

*I aim to promote evolutionary change and be a catalyst for
    growth.*

My purpose is to have a great time and laugh a lot.

PLAN BY CREATION

For most people, the word *planning* means prediction.
There's another option called *planning by creation*, and using it
can change your whole experience of creating the future.

Much of the goal setting that's done in business, government,
and education is planning by prediction. In this type of planning,
people carefully study what's happened in the past and use that
data to predict what will happen in the future.

Planning by prediction is based on a few assumptions. One is
that past events are the best predictors of what's yet to come. Another is that the forces now shaping our lives will continue to be
at work in the future. In a sense, prediction is the past masquerad-
ing as the future.

Planning by creation involves a different set of working assumptions. With this type of planning, you start from a blank slate—from nothing. Without considering the past, you state what you want to happen in the future. Then you ask how to achieve those goals. The underlying idea is that the past does not have to determine or limit what you can experience in the future.

I'm not saying that planning by creation is "better" than planning by prediction. Both types of planning have their uses. My suggestion is to know at any given moment what kind of planning you're doing—and to choose the type that suits your purpose.

An example: Two ways to create a budget

To understand the differences between planning by prediction and planning by creation, look at two ways to create a budget.

For many companies, budgeting is an exercise in planning by prediction. The corporate planners predict next year's income and expenses based on this year's income and expenses. This amounts to taking the previous year's budget and "fixing" it.

An alternative is creating a budget from scratch. This means taking last year's budget, crumpling it up, and throwing it away. Instead of fixing last year's figures, the planners ask a lot of questions: What do we value? What do we want to be doing one year from now? How much money do we want to be making? How much do we want to be spending? What steps can we take to meet these goals?

Sometimes this approach is called *zero-based budgeting*. The same process could be applied to many areas of life and be called *zero-based planning*—or planning by creation.

When planning by creation, we acknowledge that prediction is risky business. Most of us—even tea leaf readers and crystal ball gazers—are not perfectly skilled at predicting the future.

People who read the *Wall Street Journal* every day can still lose on the stock market. Political pundits can be far off base when predicting the outcome of an election.

In planning by creation, you bypass these risks. Your aim is not to predict the future, but to shape it. You think about the changes you want to see in your life, your community, your world. You imagine new results, even if they'll take five, ten, twenty, or more years to achieve.

One way to plan by creation

The following steps can get you started with planning by creation.

Step 1: Begin with a blank slate

As you prepare to create your future, be willing to completely let go of your past and current circumstances. Instead of relying on history to create your plan, erase history.

For this step, pretend that you have all the time, money, and resources you could ever want. Then ask, "What do I want to be in the future? What do I want to do? What do I want to have?"

As you ask these questions, ignore the voices that say, "You've never done anything like that. No one has ever done that before. People have always said that couldn't be done." Instead of allowing the past to place limits on you, let your imagination soar. Allow yourself to create the future from nothing.

Step 2: Design the future

Now, in your mind's eye, see yourself in the future. Describe the conditions you'd like to see in existence in twenty or more years from today.

Speak about those conditions as if they exist right now. Describe in detail what you're doing, seeing, and feeling as you stand in the future. Let those events be dynamic, multidimensional, and ever-changing. For example, you could say:

> *I'm standing in Ethiopia in the year 2020. As I look around, I see that there's plenty of food for everybody. Starvation, famine, and malnutrition are all things of the past. The land is lush and green. There's plenty of water to go around. The children are well-fed and healthy, running from house to house, laughing and playing, and they go to well-furnished schools with dedicated, patient teachers.*

In this step, create scenarios for the future that are as "far out" as possible. "Far out" has several meanings:

* *Far out in time.* For some people, this means three years from today. For others, it's three months or three centuries from now.
* *Far out in space.* Extend the range of your vision to include other people or organizations. Create goals for your company, neighborhood, city, state, nation, or planet.
* *Far out in terms of possibility.* Go for goals that might seem silly, outrageous, or even impossible at first.

Step 3: Describe the present

Now describe the present, remembering that it is as dynamic and multidimensional as the future. To get the most out of this step, be honest. Tell the truth about the present. If your design for the future includes a world free of starvation, then freely and fully admit how many people are dying of hunger today.

The purpose of this step is not to limit your vision of what is possible in the future. That would be planning by prediction.

Rather, telling the complete truth about your current reality and how it relates to the life of your dreams is a point of departure. Accurately describing the present is one way to begin creating a wonderful future.

Step 4: Link the future to the present

Now write history in advance. In your imagination, create intermediate goals by working backward from the future to the present. While doing this, continue to mentally dwell in the future. You can even assume that your preferred future has already been achieved.

Say that you envisioned the world you'd like to see in the year 2500. Now imagine what happened in the year 2400 that allowed your world to come to pass. Do the same for the years 2300, 2200, and 2100. Continue this process until you reach the present.

Return to the example of Ethiopia in the year 2020. To link that future to the present, you could create intermediate steps such as the following:

I'm in the year 2010 — the year that the problem of irrigating arid lands in this country was finally solved.

It's now 2007. A new technology that transformed this country's system of dams and reservoirs is finally in place. This technology allows farmers to store water between droughts.

Now, we're in the year 2005. We've learned ways to desalinate water from the ocean and make it available to farmers across the continent of Africa. This discovery holds the promise to transform the way food is grown and distributed.

Notice that this process proceeds in exactly the opposite direction from planning by prediction. When people set goals, they often start at the present and project forward in time. In planning by creation, you start at the future and work backward in time toward the present.

If you observe children at play, you might see them doing this kind of creation. In their make-believe worlds, children spin fantasies without any concern for "practical" questions about how to make them come true. As you experiment with planning by creation, allow yourself to regain that sense of childlike wisdom.

NOW THAT MONEY IS NO PROBLEM . . .

Imagine that you've just won a lottery with a jackpot of $5 million. If $5 million is not enough to free up your imagination, then imagine it's $5 million after taxes. If it helps, you can double or even triple the jackpot.

You now have all the money needed to sustain yourself for a lifetime. You will never have to work for money again. All your debts are paid. You have a steady stream of income extending decades into the future — enough to support any career or activity you want.

Once you've created this mental picture, describe what you will be, do, and have during the rest of your life. Do this writing for five minutes, recording as many goals as you can.

After your brainstorming session is done, review the goals you wrote. Look for any goals that you want to adopt. Also look for goals that you could meet without winning the lottery. Spot goals you could meet with only $100,000, $10,000, or $1,000. Then ask if you could meet any of these goals with no money, or with money granted to you by others.

CREATE PROJECTS FROM ABUNDANCE

Pretend that a philanthropist will pay you $100,000 per year, plus benefits, to do whatever you think will benefit your community most. What would you do? While writing, brainstorm as many answers to this question as you can.

Now imagine that a philanthropist will provide funds for you and thirty people you supervise to do something of value for the planet. You have a budget of $1 billion and 125 years to accomplish your project. What would you do? Again, write your responses.

After reviewing your answers to these two questions, think about whether they indicate any goals that you're actually willing to pursue. If so, write down those goals.

COMMIT MONEY AND TIME

This exercise offers another opportunity for you to choose how to "spend" your life energy. Writing quickly and without stopping to edit, list as many answers as possible to the following questions:

* What do I want that would take at least ten years to produce? How about twenty years? Fifty years? One hundred years?
* What do I want that would take $10,000 to produce? How about $100,000? $1 million? $1 billion?

While reviewing your answers to these questions, look for goals that you'd be willing to take on. List those goals and describe in writing your level of commitment to achieving them.

LAUNCH A PROJECT THAT WILL
BENEFIT FUTURE GENERATIONS

Throughout history, a few people conceived projects compelling enough to inspire action over many generations. The pyramids built in ancient Egypt are an example. They were conceived by pharaohs whose vision for these structures was so stunning that their descendants chose to continue the work for decades.

Another example of a multigenerational project is taking place where I live in the Black Hills of South Dakota. In 1938, the sculptor Korczak Ziolkowski envisioned a monument to the Indian chief Crazy Horse that would be carved from a mountain larger than Mount Rushmore and would stand taller than the Washington Monument. As Ziolkowski saw it, this monument and a related educational center would testify to the American Indian way of life. Ziolkowski died in 1982. Today his work is continued by his family and other people inspired by his original vision.

Take some time right now to create multigenerational goals. Describe your own "pyramids"—projects so important that others might be moved to continue them after you die. These projects could involve physical creations. They could also be social action organizations, such as Mothers Against Drunk Drivers, or business enterprises, such as a family farm.

Right now, describe ideas for a multigenerational project that you could launch. Express your ideas in writing, visual art, music, or any other appropriate medium. Create a vision that could survive you for lifetimes.

IMAGINE THAT IT'S 1985

The purpose of this exercise is to help you stretch your sense of possibility by considering some of the "impossible" goals that have been met in recent history.

To begin, mentally turn back the clock. Imagine that you're reading this book on January 1, 1985. Bring to mind some of the thoughts, feelings, and events in your life at that time.

When you've fully returned to 1985, read the following list of goals—which at the time seemed outrageous if they were to be accomplished within ten years:

* Decentralize the Soviet Union. Replace it with a number of smaller, independent states.
* End the Cold War between the United States and the Soviet Union.
* Begin closing military bases across the United States.
* Remove the Berlin Wall and reunite Germany.
* Formally end the system of apartheid and hold free, universal elections in South Africa.

Now mentally fast-forward to the present. Read over this list of goals again and remind yourself that *all of them were met within the ten-year time line.* Allow a few minutes for the reality of this fact to take hold of you.

Then, as you stand in the present moment, consider the following list of goals:

* Cut the military budget of the United States by 50 percent.
* Maintain the world population at 50 percent of its 1995 level.
* Ensure that every human being on the planet has enough food to satisfy basic nutritional requirements.

* Create a structure of international law that effectively guarantees the resolution of conflict between nations, without war.
* Create legal systems that effectively end all forms of discrimination based on age, race, ethnicity, and religion.

List any such goals that you consider possible for humanity to achieve. Add other goals as you see fit, including short-term goals that could lead to long-term goals. For those goals that you see as attainable, set a target date for each to be accomplished.

STAGE A "GOAL-AROUND"

Get together regularly with a group of people who are committed to creating the future. When you meet, ask everyone present to spend five to fifteen minutes writing goals. Then gather the participants into a circle, and ask each of them to read one goal they've written to the group. Go around the group several times, always giving people the option to pass if they choose. Postpone any debate or discussion about these goals until later. For now the idea is to nurture creativity and let people speak without fear of judgment.

Don't let the simplicity of this exercise fool you. Besides offering a learning experience, it can be uproarious fun. As you listen to others' goals, jot down ideas that sound appealing to you.

JUST OPEN YOUR MOUTH AND
SPEAK ABOUT THE FUTURE

Sometimes we don't know what we want to say until we literally open our mouths and speak about it. Powerful goals can emerge from daring, reckless verbal creation. Speaking can turn a general goal into a specific one, an abstract goal into a concrete one.

Writing down a goal is one way to make your dreams come alive. Speaking about a goal takes your desires to yet another level. When you say a goal out loud, it resonates with your voice and with your breath.

In this exercise, you will speak about your goals in the presence of another person. Find a sympathetic listener—someone who will not interrupt, question, or criticize what you say. Ask this person to take notes or run a tape recorder as you speak.

Once you've found a partner for this exercise, just talk about your goals for at least five minutes, without rehearsing or editing your thoughts. Speak even before you know what to say, and then listen to what comes out of your mouth. You can begin by saying "What I want is . . ." or "What I might do is . . ." Another option is to say "I've got several brand-new goals I've never stated to anyone before. The first goal is . . ." Then finish these sentences with as many ideas as you can create.

When your time is up, switch roles. Let the other person state her goals out loud while you listen and record them.

As you do this exercise, keep some ideas in mind:

* Quality is not an issue. Remember that you don't have to adopt or act on any of the goals that you state.
* Prepare for something wonderful and unexpected to happen.

You might come up with a goal that's never occurred to you before. You might envision a project that you'll want to take on right away.

* Maintain an environment of safety. Keep each other's goals confidential. Let the speaker be impulsive and "try on" plans without the fear of being quoted in public.

* If you notice any signs of fear or apprehension about what you'll say, just notice these feelings and continue speaking about your goals. When in doubt, just keep your lips moving.

* Stand up as you state your goals. Many of us think better on our feet.

* As you speak, allow completely new goals to emerge—no preconceptions, no agendas, no limits. Don't worry about telling the other person what he or she wants to hear. Simply express your greatness.

* If you get stuck during this exercise, read or recall a few goals you've written before. Or keep repeating the words "I also want . . ." and completing the sentence with whatever comes to mind.

Do this exercise regularly with people you know well and those you hardly know at all. Gradually lengthen the amount of time you spend speaking of goals. Go from five minutes to ten, fifteen, twenty, or even more minutes.

This kind of speaking is like continuously writing goals. Both techniques can help us access reserves of creativity and take us to deeper levels of knowing. Listening with full, permissive attention to another person's wishes for the future is an empowering and unusual gift.

ASK SOMEONE ELSE TO
CREATE YOUR FUTURE

As one path to uncovering more creative goals, experiment with letting another person create your future.

If this seems like an invitation to turn your life over to another or to let someone else violate your privacy, then remember that people set goals for each other all the time. Teachers set goals for their students. Parents set goals for their children. Salespeople set goals for their customers, and employers set goals for their employees. Letting other people set goals for you does not mean that you will automatically accept them.

Other people will likely bring up goals that have never occurred to you—goals that may inspire your passionate and lifelong commitment. Remember that you can keep all the other person's ideas, use only a few of them, or throw them all away after this exercise is done.

1. Choose a person to be your partner for this exercise. Set a time and a place to meet. This person might be a friend, family member, coworker, or relative stranger.
2. Ask this person, "If you were going to live my life, what would you do, have, and be?" Let the other person speak for at least five minutes while you record goals in many different areas.
3. To get the most out of this exercise, practice nonjudgmental listening. Reacting defensively defeats the purpose, which is to practice creative thinking. This kind of thinking flourishes in an atmosphere of total candor and acceptance. If you hear a goal that confuses or angers you, just notice your reaction. Then return your attention to listening.

CREATE SOMEONE ELSE'S FUTURE

You can write goals for other people—even if these people are not present when you do so, or even if they have no idea that you'd like to help create their future. Just write each person's name, along with one goal for that person. If you think of more than one goal, great. Write down those goals also.

Now you have several options for dealing with the goals you've created. One is to share your goals with the people involved. Another is to simply ask these people to change their behavior in a way that's consistent with your goals. (You don't have to tell them about the goals you've written.) You could also choose to keep the goals to yourself and not share them with anyone.

Over the coming months, keep track of the goals you've set for other people and how many of them are fulfilled. You might find that the people who know nothing of your goals for them still meet those goals anyway!

WORK WITH YOUR SECRETS

To begin this exercise, create an environment of safety. Find a place where you can be alone. Plan to write your responses on 3×5 cards or paper that you can destroy later.

Now list your secrets. Write down everything you don't want others to know about you. Look at all aspects of your life: money, sex, work, mistakes, lies, crimes, and whatever else comes to mind. Remember that secrets can also include accomplishments that you've kept to yourself.

Once you have listed all of your secrets, put them into the

following categories. If your secrets are on cards, organize them in several different piles. If they are on paper, mark them as follows:

* Circle the secrets that you might be willing to reveal by speaking directly to the person involved.
* Underline the secrets that you might be willing to reveal by speaking to someone other than the person directly involved.
* Put an asterisk by the secrets that you wish to do something about, even though you want them to remain secret. Think about whether you'd be willing to make amends to the people involved or take some other action to diminish the consequences of keeping the secret.
* Draw a line through the secrets that you plan to do nothing about and that you wish to remain secret.

Next, choose which secrets you intend to turn into goals. Consider the advantages of revealing each secret or making amends, and include a time line for taking these actions.

Return to this exercise periodically, and consider circling, underlining, or highlighting any of the secrets you've marked with an asterisk. Also write goals for how you want to handle secrets in the future.

CLIMB THE MOUNTAINTOP

This exercise offers one way to discover what you truly value. There are four steps to complete.

Step 1

Imagine that you're about to climb to the top of a mountain, dig a hole, and bury something in that hole for posterity. Consider the legacy that you'd like to leave the world. Choose something you'd like archaeologists to discover decades from now. Possibilities include an inspiring quote or saying, an essay, a poem, a work of art, an account of a mistake and what you learned from it, a list of personal characteristics you value, or a memorial to a relationship. Ask, "What object or symbol of myself do I want to leave behind when I die?" Put your answer in writing.

Step 2

Now describe what you want to *release* from your life and the world as you climb to the mountaintop. Examples include fears, worries, resentments, or personal shortcomings. You can describe these in writing or another medium, such as drawing, music, or clay sculpture. Think of these as objects to burn or bury in the side of the mountain so that no one will ever see them again. These are aspects of your past that you want to be done with forever.

Step 3

Next, describe in writing or another medium what you want to carry *down* from the mountaintop. Choose something that you want to make a part of your life from now on—perhaps a quality you want to bring to your relationships, a personal characteristic, or a list of values you will act on every day.

If possible, carry out the first three steps literally. That is, create the objects you've described and bury them in an actual mountain or hill.

Step 4

After completing the first three steps, look for ideas you can turn into goals. For instance, you could set a goal to release specific resentments or adopt new habits that are consistent with your values. Record these goals.

YOUR DREAM CAREER

Describe what you'd do if you could work in any career without having to prepare for it.

Imagine that the people closest to you—family, friends, coworkers—have become suddenly enlightened. They will give you unconditional support, both emotional and financial, to do whatever you choose.

As of today, you also possess whatever skills you need in order to achieve your goals. If you're a "wanna-be" rock star who can't carry a tune, great. You now possess a thunderous, stunning voice. If you always wanted to be a surgeon but never could invest in the necessary training, no problem. You are now a surgeon on a par with the greatest in the world.

Look to see if any other constraints in your life prevent you from doing what you want to do. This could be anything that you see as a limitation: your size, gender, race, nationality, physical ability, or anything else. Simply imagine that these limits no longer exist. Don't worry about *how* to make this happen. Just play with the possibilities.

Now that you have the skills, support, time, and money to do whatever you want, describe your dream career in writing.

When you're done writing, ask, "What's interesting to me

about this career? And, how could I make this interest part of my life *without* retraining?" For example, if you love to sing, you could join a church choir without training to become a professional musician. Also consider the possibility that you could actually attain your dream career.

Now write any goals that occurred to you while doing this exercise.

GUIDED IMAGERY FOR
CREATING YOUR FUTURE

This exercise is designed to release your creative powers and help you tap into your subconscious wisdom. Included are a series of statements to bring you to a state of relaxed alertness. Then there are suggestions to help you explore many aspects of your life and create goals related to them.

Ask someone else to read the following script to you, or tape-record it so you can play it back later. Throughout the script you'll see ellipses (. . .). These indicate spots for the reader to pause for a bit.

Before you begin, get a pencil and some 3×5 cards so that you can write down goals at the end of the guided imagery. Intend to invent a future filled with the most happiness, health, love, and wealth that you can imagine.

The following is the script for this guided imagery. Feel free to rewrite this script to fit the particular circumstances of your life.

For the next several minutes prepare to contact a part of you that can create empowering, affirming goals for all aspects of your life. This part of you may be hidden from your ordinary consciousness. Prepare to tap a source of inner wisdom. . . .

During this exercise, allow yourself to relax completely while still continuing to listen to my voice. If you notice yourself drifting off to sleep, gently bring yourself back to a waking state. . . .

To begin, gently allow yourself to relax even as you remain alert. Whether you're sitting or lying down, keep your spine straight. . . . Allow the energy in your body to circulate freely as you relax and listen to the sound of my voice. . . . Allow a deeper part of you to come to the surface. . . . Ask this part of you what it knows about your life purpose and goals . . . .

When it feels right, let your eyes close. . . . Or, if you prefer, keep your eyes open and gently focus on a point in front of you. . . .

As you continue to relax, be aware of your breath. Notice your breathing without seeking to change it in any way. Just notice the air as it enters your body and leaves your body. . . . When it feels right, let your breathing become slower and deeper. . . .

As you relax, let your muscles begin to melt, like butter on a summer day. Notice what supports your body—the chair or the floor. . . . Notice where the chair or floor supports you. Just allow this source of support to hold you as you release any remaining tension. . . .

Now gently bring your attention to the soles of your feet. . . . If your attention drifts, gently return it to the soles of your feet. . . . Then let your attention move slowly to your ankles, lower legs, and knees. . . . Notice any feelings of tension or discomfort there. . . . Allow those feelings to dissolve and melt away. . . . Do the same as you gently scan your thighs . . . your hips . . . and now your abdomen. . . . Let your belly become soft and heavy and warm as beautiful feelings of relaxation flow through this area of your body. . . . Allow those same feelings to flow around and through your back and up through your chest . . . now through your neck and shoulders . . . and now all the way down and through your arms. . . .

Now, as you allow yourself to relax more deeply, bring your attention to the palms of your hands. . . . If your attention wanders, gently return it to the palms of your hands. . . . Your hands are becoming softer and warmer and heavier with each moment. . . . You feel absolutely wonderful. . . .

While you allow your entire body to relax even more, bring your awareness to your mouth and jaw. . . . Allow any hint of tension there to flow out of your body. . . . Let the muscles of your mouth, jaw, face, and forehead soften. . . .

As your body reaches an even deeper level of relaxation, gently scan your entire body for any remaining feelings of tension. . . . Allow those feelings to dissolve. . . . It's safe to release them now. . . . Now, you are more comfortable than you've been in a long, long time. . . . You are complete and whole. . . . You can open up to your experience, moment by moment, knowing that whatever happens is for your highest good. . . .

At this moment, know that your mind has become capable of revealing what it knows at a very deep level. . . . You can now open up to a powerful state of mind that always lies within you. . . .

In the next few minutes, you will gently turn your attention to several areas of your life. . . . As you do this, let your desires for each of these areas come to the surface. . . . At first, no images or words may come to mind. . . . That's fine. . . . Or you may find that a whole flood of images and words comes to mind. . . . That is also fine. . . . There is no need for you to

direct or consciously create thoughts and images. . . . Just al-
low them to surface as they choose. . . .

Now, while considering your family, *what would you like*
to see in the future? . . . Think about the future you want for
your mother . . . your father . . . your brothers or sisters . . . your
spouse . . . your children . . . grandparents . . . aunts or uncles.
. . . What do you envision for each of these people?

Now, regarding your friends, *what do you want to see in*
your future? . . . Consider your enemies *and what you envision*
in the future for them. . . .

Consider your sexual life *and what you would like to expe-*
rience for yourself and your partner in the future. . . .

As you continue to relax, please consider your health. . . .
What would you like to see in this area of life in the future? . . .
What will you do to enjoy the benefits of exercise . . . of health-
ful nutrition . . . of a life that's free of distress? . . .

Now, while considering another area of life—your finances—*what would you like to see in your future? . . .*

Now think about your home. . . . *What do you want to see*
in your home for the future? . . . How about the car *you drive?*
. . . What other possessions should be part of your life in the fu-
ture? . . .

Now regarding your career, *consider what you would like*
to do or be in the future. . . .

As you relax even more deeply, allow your natural knowing
to take place. . . . Let your deep mind reveal a future that you
can care about passionately . . . .

Now, think about what you want to see in your relationships at work . . . *in your* education . . . *in your* spiritual development . . . *in your* leisure . . . *for your* entertainment . . . *in*
your artistic expression . . . *singing . . . painting . . . sculpture*
. . . poetry . . . dance . . . in your hobbies. . . .

Now gently turn your attention to the world beyond your immediate personal life. . . . Consider the contributions you'd like to make to your neighborhood . . . your city . . . your state . . . your country . . . and your planet . . . to the human family as a whole. . . . In each of these areas, envision what you'd like to see in the long-range future. . . .

Next, turn your awareness to the environment, *and consider what changes you would like to see in the future. . . .*

Also see your death. *. . . Imagine how you want your death to take place. . . . See what you will be doing just before you die and who will be with you. . . . Notice how other people remember you. . . . See how they celebrate your contribution to their lives. . . . Hear what they say about you. . . .*

As you consider all these aspects of your life and more, what other positive changes do you see occurring in your future? . . . Just let your attention dwell on this question for several minutes. . . .

Now fully and completely allow your desires to surface in any area *that comes to your mind, even if it has already been mentioned. . . . Create what you want to see in each area as it occurs to you. . . . Allow your deep mind to speak its full wisdom to you. . . .*

You have been in a deeply relaxed state for some time. . . . Now gradually return your awareness to the room you are in . . . and to the floor or chair that supports you. . . . You can now gently bring yourself back to waking consciousness. . . . When it feels right to you, slowly allow your eyes to open. . . . And now you can gently stretch your arms and legs. . . . If you choose, slowly rise to a standing position and stretch even more. . . .

Now spend five minutes writing down whatever goals come to mind. . . . Don't censor any thoughts. . . . Rather, just allow what you've learned from your deeper self to come to your everyday consciousness. . . . See these goals as a sacred creation. Consider sharing your goals with another person, someone you care deeply about. In each moment remember that you can access the wisdom of your deep mind at any time, staying in touch with the infinite possibilities for your future.

LOOK FORWARD TO THE "BEST YEARS OF YOUR LIFE"

Imagine that you are now age eighteen and just graduating from high school. As a new graduate, describe what you plan to do with the rest of your life. Record your goals.

Then mentally return to the present and review what you've written. Look for any goals that you still want to achieve, and add these to the ones you've already created.

As you jot down these goals, notice any feelings of regret or thoughts that you've "missed the boat" on getting what you want in life. It's never too late to set and meet goals. In creating the future, you could discover that the best years of your life are still ahead of you.

TURN YOUR VISIONS INTO VISUALS

One way to keep your vision clear and compelling is to represent it visually. Creating diagrams, drawings, charts, and other illustrations allows you to create new goals and arrange hundreds of existing goals into organized patterns. Then you can track your progress and make daily choices based on the "big picture"—a comprehensive image of what you want.

You have many options for creating a personal picture of the life you desire. One is the lifeline included earlier in this chapter. Other kinds of visuals are described here. You can change them, combine them, or create new kinds of your own.

"Tree" diagrams

Tree diagrams resemble the organizational charts used by businesses to indicate each employee's position in the company. You can use a similar type of diagram to represent your life plan.

Inside the top box in this diagram, list the main topic. For example, you could write your life purpose, core values, or career goal. You could also describe a major project, such as building an addition to your home. At the next level, include major categories of your plan. For each succeeding level, list appropriate subcategories. An example follows.

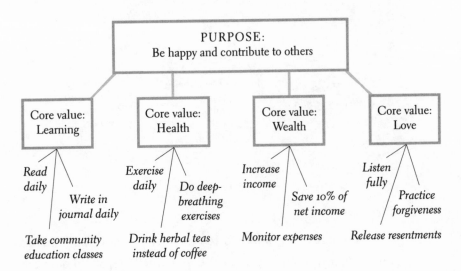

Tree diagrams offer ways to help you break larger goals, projects, and activities into smaller elements and see how each element relates to the others.

Circle diagrams

Another way to keep returning to the big picture of your life is to organize key areas in your life—such as important relationships and major projects—in circles. The size of each circle can represent the amount of time, money, or effort that you want to devote to each area. A sample is shown here:

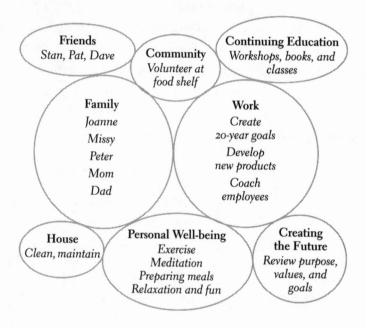

Pie charts

Pie charts offer a way to represent the relative amounts of time, money, or other resources that you will devote to different aspects of your life. Draw a circle ("pie") that represents the total amount of time you have available. Then "cut" pieces of the pie to represent the approximate amounts of time you will devote to various activities.

An early draft of my life plan included this chart:

Computer software

You can find computer software to create the visuals described in this section and many other kinds. Examples include software for drawing, painting, database management, outlining, and project management. Other software can help you create critical path diagrams, a sophisticated type of chart used to schedule long-term projects in business and industry. All of these tools can help you keep first things first as you create the life of your dreams.

CREATE A MIND MAP

One visual tool you might enjoy is a mind map. This method of representing ideas comes from the work of Tony Buzan and is now used by students and people in many professions. Many find that mind maps are an ideal to way to record their vision of the future.

To create a mind map, begin with these steps:

1. Get a blank, unlined sheet of paper. The standard letter size is fine, though you might wish to use a larger sheet. Orient the paper horizontally.

2. Choose the main topic, or "hub," for your mind map. Express this topic in one to three key words, and write those words in the center of the page. Key words capture an image or concept in the fewest words possible—usually concrete nouns or active verbs. For example, the phrase "My goals for 1999" could be written simply as "Goals 2000."

3. Now record subtopics using key words, just as you did for the hub of your mind map. Place these subtopics in branches radiating from the hub. Say that a number of your goals for 2000 relate to health. Write the key word Health, and connect it with a line to the hub.

4. Continue writing key words that express related ideas. If one of your health-related goals for 2000 is to exercise daily, you could write Exercise and connect it with a line to the key word Health. Then write Daily and connect it to the key word Exercise.

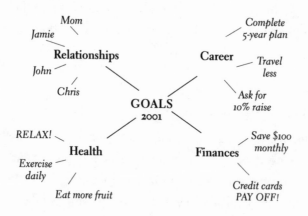

That's it. If you can do this much, you've mastered the basics of mind mapping. You can make your map even more engaging by using color, designs, and pictures. For instance, record all your health-related goals in green and work-related goals in red. And instead of writing Exercise, draw a picture of yourself jogging.

To get the most benefit from this exercise, keep creating mind maps. Post them in places where you'll see them often—on your desk, a wall, or even a bathroom mirror.

PLANT SEEDS FOR
CREATING YOUR FUTURE

Powerful goals can be revealed to us as we sleep. We experience an altered state of consciousness just before we fall asleep. While in this state, we can be open to suggestions that enhance our creativity and influence our dreams.

For example, John Robbins got the idea to write his book *Diet for a New America* while dreaming. He saw images of animals that talked to him about the relationship between human beings and the rest of the natural world. The animals advised Robbins to write about this topic. The result was an eloquent book about vegetarianism that was nominated for a Pulitzer Prize.

You can take advantage of this phenomenon to plant the seeds for effective goals. Tonight, shortly before you go to sleep, repeat the following sentence to yourself: "I will rest soundly and dream of new possibilities."

You could also add these ideas: "I will awake refreshed with many new opportunities for my life. I will remember what I dream."

Tomorrow morning, describe your dreams in writing as soon as possible after waking up. Then immediately write down any goals that occur to you.

HARVEST YOUR DREAMS

Here is a more detailed process for turning dream images into goals. Think of a vivid dream you've had recently. Then write about it using the seven steps that follow.

1. Describe the dream in as much detail as you can remember.
2. Give the dream a title.
3. Speak or write about the images in your dream (animals, people, objects, materials) as if you were from another planet and were seeing these things for the first time. You have no familiar names to give these images. Just describe in detail what you see, using precise adjectives. For example, spilled house paint might be a thick, sticky, flowing liquid. (Such descriptions might allow you to find meaning in an image that common terminology might mask.)
4. Describe the feelings you had when you awoke and remembered your dream.
5. Translate your dream into real life. In other words, look for what your dream reminds you of in your waking life. The thick, sticky, flowing liquid might relate to your feelings of being "stuck in the mud"—blocked in some area of your life, such as a relationship or your career.
6. Assume for a moment that there might be some message in your dream from your subconscious mind. Explore what that message might be. State it in one sentence. Perhaps

there is more than one message. Write down the other messages also.

7. Write whatever goals seem appropriate, given the messages of your dream.

CREATE THE WORLD'S FUTURE

If you are a leader—or if you want to become a leader—please spend time creating the future. Leaders in the past rose to greatness on the wings of their dreams, creating visions that inspired the people around them.

Though some people became leaders almost by accident, many took the time to create and communicate a vision for the long-range, global future. Micah, a leading prophet of ancient Israel whose words are recorded in the Old Testament, envisioned a world where swords were turned into plowshares and nations abandoned war. In more recent history, Mikhail Gorbachev's vision of a nuclear-free, nonviolent world led to perestroika and many new freedoms in the former USSR. Marian Wright Edelman's vision of a safe world for all children created a new organization with global impact, the Children's Defense Fund. These are just a few examples.

Much of this book is written for individuals who want to create a more wonderful life for themselves. In addition, the ideas I suggest are easily applied in many larger arenas. My goal is that by 2010, leaders of major businesses, educational institutions, and governments will routinely create written plans that extend decades into the future. And my desire is to write and speak in ways that move leaders and potential leaders around the world to invent dramatic futures for our planet. I want these people to invent blueprints for the distant future that are clearly worthy of our time and energy.

Today this kind of vision is rare. Companies are often led by people focused on the next quarter's bottom line. Universities are frequently led by people who can picture what they want only for the next academic year. Politicians often concentrate on the next election. Seldom do leaders create a long-range, multidecade or even multicentury dream to inspire us.

As leaders, we can dramatically increase our effectiveness by taking time to create the future. We can take responsibility for the lack of motivation in the people around us. We can help them move into action by speaking about a vision of the future that is worthy of their enthusiasm. Without a long-term motive, people can find their motivation missing.

As the leader of an organization, do the same thing that you do as the "leader" of your personal life: Invent a vision—plans, goals, and purposes—worthy of constant focus. If you're a manager and conclude that your employees are performing below standard, articulate a powerful mission. If you're a politician and discover that most of the electorate does not vote, then take it upon yourself to speak of a compelling dream for your nation and your world.

CREATE THE NEXT
TEN THOUSAND YEARS

Extending your goals outward in time—as far as you can possibly imagine—is one way to create a comprehensive, global vision. There's no need to stop at setting goals for ten, twenty, fifty, or one hundred years. Your goals can extend five hundred, one thousand, or even ten thousand years into the future.

If thinking so far ahead seems like an impossible or useless mental stretch, then keep a few things in mind:

* In the entire span of human history, a century is a very short period of time. Recall the history courses you took in school. There you probably reviewed entire decades in a matter of minutes. You can now preview the distant future in the same way that you reviewed the distant past.
* Goals for the distant future can represent highlights, not detailed agendas. When you set goals for the next decade or next century, you will mostly create the major events—the turning points in human affairs. These transformational events might take place over a period of many years.
* When you think five hundred years or more into the future, it's easier to stretch your vision beyond short-term self-interest. In five hundred years you will be gone from the earth. So will your children, your grandchildren, and their grandchildren. From this long-range perspective, you can be more objective and consider the fate of humanity as a whole.
* After thinking in long stretches of time, you might find it easier to think about shorter stretches. Once you've practiced thinking one hundred, five hundred, and even ten thousand years into the future, the notion of planning five years, ten years, and even twenty years into the future can seem like child's play.

With the previous points in mind, complete the following steps:

1. Describe the world you want to see in the year 2500. Remember that this is not an exercise in predicting the world of 2500.

Rather, it's a statement about what you want humanity to achieve by that time.

2. After you've played with creating the world of 2500, go even farther out in the future. Conceive the world you'd like to see in the year 3000 or 5000.

3. Now stretch your planning muscles even more, and write goals for the year 10,000. Remember that ten thousand years ago, people were not yet farming, let alone writing.

To fully experience the excitement of such long-range goal setting, do this exercise with others. Working individually, spend ten minutes writing goals for the year 2500. At the end of that time, ask all present to share one of their goals with the group. If there's time, go around the room several times. Agree to let everyone contribute a goal without fear of criticism. If you hear a goal that seems off track, you can later modify the goal so that it works for you and offer it to the group.

After you've completed this group exercise, list the goals you heard that interest you the most. To get full benefit, do it several times.

This concept of long-range goal setting might seem strange to you right now. If so, that's fine. Just experiment with the idea and see if it has any potential usefulness for you.

Some goals for the year 10,000

Consider the following list of goals from one group of people who mentally stood in the year 10,000 and described what they saw:

We can decode natural communication systems. Now
humans can communicate with rocks, plants, and all

species of animals. The birds consistently tell us, "Don't worry. Be happy." (And when the birds talk, people listen.)

Eating is optional; we eat only for pleasure. It's a world of virtual cuisine.

Physical pain is erased with thought.

Bodies are optional, and we can live in the spiritual dimension at any time. There are "bodies optional" beaches.

War has been absent from Earth for centuries. Now conflict is resolved by teams of skilled negotiators who can be dispatched to any place on the planet in a matter of seconds—before any dispute can involve weapons.

Cities are limited in size to 100,000 people at most. This, combined with nonpolluting, clean, and safe mass transit, makes traffic congestion and vehicle accidents a thing of the distant past.

Natural disasters are predicted with absolute accuracy, far enough in advance to make mass evacuations possible. No longer is anyone killed because of tornadoes, floods, or earthquakes.

Prisons have been eliminated, replaced by strictly supervised programs in which people who commit crimes work to make amends to their victims.

Education at all levels—from kindergarten to postgraduate school—is universal and free.

We can communicate with the surviving spirit of any being who has ever lived on the planet. This greatly reduces the sadness associated with death.

CREATE THE FUTURE FROM NOTHING

This exercise is an open inquiry into what's possible for the rest of your life . . . and beyond. During the exercise, you will experiment with totally erasing your personal history and current identity. You will start your life over again and then set goals.

Please be willing to stick with this process even if it sounds crazy. There is a logic hidden in beginning your life from nothing. Most of us live full lives, filled with a lot of "something." We carry around a detailed personal history: successes, failures, attachments, obligations, requirements, relationships, careers, thoughts, feelings, habits, and much more.

We can become so committed to preserving our personal history that we squash any possibility of change. Often history has such unrelenting momentum that we forget about alternatives. Our lives can get so "full" that we leave no room for something fresh—like a room that is so full that it has no place for a beautiful new painting.

So, consider what it would be like to re-create your life from a clean slate. Imagine that you could wipe out the past and start over afresh. What would you do? What would you have? Who would you choose to be?

To create a blank slate, relax, and right now, while you are reading, imagine doing the following:

* Erase your current job. Imagine that you have no job. Whether you love it, hate it, or feel neutral about it, the job's gone. Vanished. (Relax. You can have your job back at the end of this exercise.)
* Erase your financial concerns. Money problems are permanently behind you. Imagine that money is no longer used as a medium of exchange. Banks and credit cards no longer

exist. There's no point in having money, and no one has any. Money is gone.

* Erase your health problems. Disease, chronic illness, and disability—whether real or imagined—are no longer issues for you.

* Erase your friends. Peers, colleagues, neighbors, acquaintances—all of them are gone. (Don't worry about being lonely. Your friends will still be there after this exercise.)

* Erase your enemies. Imagine that any people you resented or fought with are no longer part of your life.

* Erase your family. (Again, don't worry. These people are safe, and you can bring them back later.) For now, pretend that they are no longer around.

* Erase your spouse or romantic partner. Do this now, even if you have a wonderful relationship. Let this person go to the same place that your friends and family have gone.

* Erase your house or apartment. Imagine that you have no place to live. No longer do you define yourself by the size, price, or location of your living space.

* Erase your other possessions, especially the big-ticket items such as cars or boats. And erase your precious possessions as well—the pictures, jewelry, old letters, and keepsakes.

* Erase your community. The town, city, or rural area where you grew up is gone. So is the town where you currently live.

* Erase your memories. All those accomplishments, those hurts, those mistakes, those successes—release them all.

* Release your expectations. Erase any thoughts about how future events should unfold.

* Erase time. Mentally toss your watch and clocks out the window. Then erase the window.

* Erase your values. Release any goal to be wise, healthy, creative, wealthy, passionate, punctual, or polite. Also let go of

any goals about what you'd like to do or have in your lifetime.

* Erase your religion. For the moment, pretend there's no need for any special set of beliefs or practices.

* Now notice anything about yourself that remains. Is your body still there? Erase it. Are your clothes or glasses still there? Erase them, too. (Notice that you erased your body before you erased your clothes so there's no need to feel embarrassed.) Also erase your emotions, opinions, and thoughts. If you have any worry about all that you've erased so far, just notice that worry and erase it also. Then erase anything else that's left.

* Finally, notice any remaining thoughts about this exercise — that it's silly, profound, boring, frightening, or anything else. Let those thoughts billow up and vanish like a bubble.

If these suggestions worked for you, you've arrived at a blank slate. Congratulations.

You've arrived at a peak state of creativity. In fact, now that you're nobody, you may even be better company than when you were merely somebody. At this moment, you're free to make any choice whatsoever about what to be, do, and have. From the state of nothingness, you can call forth all possibilities.

Dwell in this state for at least five minutes. You could even extend this time to several hours. While in this state, ask yourself, "What do I want? What's next for me?" Write your answers as goals.

After you've recorded these goals, slowly let yourself start to fill up again. Allow all your old roles, relationships, and posses-sions to *gradually* rejoin you. Return yourself to the present.

When you've fully come back to the present, review the goals you wrote when you were nothing. Save those goals to review and refine as you read the rest of this book.

Step 3:
Construct

*You know the story of the three brick masons.
When the first man was asked what he was building,
he answered gruffly, without even raising his eyes from
his work, "I'm laying bricks." The second man replied,
"I'm building a wall." But the third man said enthusiastically
and with obvious pride, "I'm building a cathedral."*

—Margaret M. Stevens

FOUR PATHS TO MORE POWERFUL GOALS

Doing the exercises so far in this book probably has left you with a large collection of goals, perhaps hundreds of them. Now you can gather those ideas, organize them, refine them, and turn them into a comprehensive plan for your life.

To enhance the power of your goals, consider adding the following four items to them:

* Time lines
* Priorities
* Categories
* Partners

In discussing these items, I'll describe a way to include them on the 3×5 cards that already contain goals. On the following page is the basic format.

If you're recording your goals in a bound journal, on a computer, or in some other medium, find ways to include these four items with your goals.

ADD TIME LINES

On each card, in the upper left-hand corner, assign a time line to the goal. Adding a time line to a goal will raise your level of commitment to it. Many people report that when they add time lines, their goals suddenly become more concrete and attainable.

There are several options for stating time lines. Here are some examples:

By (date)
Until (date)
From (date) to (date)
Number of hours

Note that a goal without a time line can still be powerful. Some goals are more effective with no time line at all. That's true of "Be loving" or "Practice forgiveness." You probably wouldn't want to limit such goals with a time line: "I will be loving on Tuesday afternoons. I will practice forgiveness until I turn fifty."

Instead, you can write the word *ongoing* in the upper left-hand corner of your cards or just leave the area blank.

You might feel stumped when choosing a time line. No problem. If you're in doubt, just make up any date or range of dates that comes to mind. And if the time line looks off base once you write it down, then just change it. Even when an initial time line misses the mark, it helps you choose a more accurate one.

With practice, you'll gain skill at estimating the number of hours, days, or weeks needed to meet a goal. You might find that when you limit the amount of time for a project—set fewer hours than you first estimate—that time appears more precious and you're likely to use it effectively.

ADD PRIORITIES

Not all the goals you create will be equally important. Accomplishing some of them will create more value for you than others. In order to get the most out of your efforts, assign priorities. I suggest that you write a priority for the goal in the upper right-hand corner of each card. You could begin doing this right now.

There are several options for assigning priorities. *Letters of the alphabet* offer a tried and true way. In the ABC system, the most important and urgent goals receive an A rating (your promises) and less urgent, less important goals receive a B (your plans) or a C (possibilities).

You could also add an O (for obligation) next to the priority on each goal, to distinguish those goals you are taking on because you think you *should* from those you really *want* to achieve. You might want to minimize the number of goals with an O.

If you choose this system, watch for that universal syndrome—C fever. This is the compelling urge to chip away at the easy, low-priority tasks and avoid the more challenging, high-priority tasks. A more powerful alternative is to "work your A's off."

You can also use *numbers*. For example, rate each goal on a scale from 1 to 100. Goals assigned numbers between 1 and 30 can be possibilities (equivalent to C priorities). Goals in the 31-60 range can be plans (B priorities), and those numbered 61-100 can be promises (A priorities). Using numbers allows you to prioritize within the three main number ranges. For example, a goal rated as 95 is higher priority than one rated as 90, even though both fall within the top priority range.

There's no problem with having an excess of goals rated 30 or below. Giving yourself permission to write these goals can clear a mental path for the 90s, 95s, and the 100s.

Another option is simple *rank ordering*. Here you number goals in order of their importance. Goal number one is what you'll do first (the most important), followed by goal number two, goal number three, and so on.

An additional method is to assign priority with *words*. For example, each of the following statements signals a level of priority, going from lowest to highest:

* "I *might* accomplish this goal." In this case, you like the idea and want to include the goal in your life plan. You consider it a possibility. But though you think the goal is a good idea, you're not yet committed to getting it accomplished.
* "I *want* to accomplish this goal." These words reveal that the goal is something you desire, even something you feel passionately about—a more intense level of emotion than *might*. The goal is something that's attractive and appealing to you, but not something you're willing to guarantee yet.
* "I *plan* to accomplish this goal." The word *plan* reveals a

higher level of commitment than *might* or *want*. Although plans are not guarantees, these goals are more likely to be accomplished. You've invested thinking, writing, and action in this goal—a higher level of commitment than that implied by the word *want*.

* "I *promise* to accomplish this goal." Promises represent the highest level of commitment. These words have the weight of a marriage vow. In effect, you're saying, "You can absolutely count on me to get this done. I'm willing to stake my reputation on it. I give you my word."

ADD CATEGORIES AND SUBCATEGORIES

Before you feel overwhelmed by the sheer number of your goals, take a few minutes to create a list of five to seven major categories for them. Then sort your goals into these categories.

No single list of categories makes sense for everyone. Choose a set of topics that works for you. Here are some examples:

* Career
* Children
* Community
* Contribution
* Education
* Environment
* Family
* Finances
* Friendships
* Fun

* Growth and development
* Health
* Hobbies
* Living space
* Spiritual life
* Values and beliefs

Organizational plans could include different categories, such as facilities, research, personnel, marketing, sales, and advertising.

Write categories in the lower left-hand corner of your cards. You could also write these categories on dividers, place the dividers in a 3×5 card box, and place each goal in the appropriate category.

After you've created five to seven major categories, then add subcategories—and then even sub-subcategories. For instance, the major category *health* could include the subcategories *diet*, *exercise*, and *stress management*. And any of these subcategories could include sub-subcategories. *Stress management*, for example, could include *relaxation techniques* and *support groups*.

ADD PARTNERS

In the lower right-hand corner of your card (or somewhere next to your goal in your journal or computer list), note your partners in accomplishing this goal. People can support you in many different ways as you move toward your goal. They may include friends, family members, colleagues, teachers, foundations, people to whom you can delegate tasks, support groups, organizations, and more.

Write the name of these partners on your card. For one goal, you might write *Delegated to Melissa* in the lower right-hand corner. For another goal, you could write *Ask Bill*, or *Contact Rotary Club*. If you're on your own with a particular goal, then leave this space blank or write the word *self*.

Choose partners with care. When they keep their word and carry out their part of the plan, partners can be powerful allies. And if they forget or fail to do what you ask, you could miss your goal by a mile.

As you create the life of your dreams, there's no reason to go it alone. Ask for help. Other people could be as thrilled about some of your goals as you are. In the process of meeting your goals, you could greatly expand your support system. Creating the future can be an exercise in creating community as well.

DO WHAT WORKS

Remember that the suggestion to list time lines, priorities, categories, and partners is just that—a suggestion. You might choose to let some goals stand without any of these elements. Add these four elements when they help clarify your thinking and move you into action.

Above all, keep creating new goals. You can always come back later to add one of these elements.

By 12/31/99 B	Ongoing A	6/99–6/00 90
Buy a new car	Be more assertive	Lose 24 pounds
Finances Expenses New items Doug	Values Self	Health Weight Stan

Ongoing #1	By 7/15 Promise	1 hour Plan
Be more candid	Have more unscheduled time	Get a faster computer
Values Speaking Self	Fun Joanne	Work Delegated to Peter

REARRANGE YOUR GOALS

An advantage of assigning time lines, priorities, categories, and partners to your goals is that you can sort goals according to any of these elements. You could have dividers in your card box for goals you intend to accomplish in January or February, or by the year 2000 or 2001.

You could also sort goals by *roles* (goals that relate to your activities as a parent, friend, family member, professional, homemaker, volunteer, or student) or *arenas of activity* (personal, professional, political, and spiritual).

Sorting your goals in new ways allows you to spot any lack of balance in your vision. For instance, after sorting your goals by time line, you might discover that you have few goals that go beyond twenty years into the future. You can balance your vision by writing more goals that extend beyond twenty years. Or you could find that you have too many goals in a category labeled *do today*. Noticing this, you can complete some goals within longer time frames, such as a month or a year.

Using 3 × 5 cards to record your goals makes it easy to reorder them in many ways. You can reshuffle your cards according to new categories or time frames. Writing goals on a computer offers similar flexibility.

Please experiment with this suggestion now. Rearrange your goals in a variety of ways. Look for any gaps in your vision of the future, and write goals to fill in those gaps.

FINE-TUNE YOUR FUTURE

Skilled writers seldom stop with the first draft. By producing a number of drafts, writers gain opportunities to sharpen word choice, delete unnecessary sentences, and fix gaps in logic.

You can gain the same benefit as you become the "author" of the rest of your life. Revising the first draft of your goals can make them more complete, specific, focused, and easy to meet.

As you fine-tune your future, keep the following suggestions in mind. They can apply to the second, third, or hundredth draft of any life plan.

Add more details

You can give your goals more impact by loading them with details. Just answer some questions about each goal:

* What is the specific outcome I desire?
* When will I accomplish this goal?
* Where will I accomplish this goal?
* Who can help me accomplish this goal?
* What are some possible obstacles to meeting this goal?
* How can I overcome those obstacles?

Details can actually increase your range of possibilities. Say that you add a small detail to your plan, such as the goal "Improve my health by eating less fat." Now you can brainstorm ways to reduce fat such as buying low-fat foods, eating out less, reading labels more often, and so on. These added details open up other goals relating to health.

When your vision of the future is rich in specifics, you're more likely to get what you want.

Check for alignment

Take a break to step back and check for overall consistency in your goals. See if your goals are aligned with one another and with your life purpose.

If a person who values frugality also has a goal to own fifty pairs of shoes, goal conflict is occurring. This kind of contradiction leads to muddy thinking and confused action.

Translate your vision into a new format

Your vision of the future can take many forms. If you haven't been using 3×5 cards, consider putting your future into a box of these cards. If you have been using 3×5 cards, then consider translating them into a formal written document resembling a legal contract or into a visual, nonverbal form—charts, colorful diagrams, or three-dimensional models that architects use. A computer database program that can sort goals by many different criteria offers another option.

Choosing new formats in which to cast your goals will let your creativity flourish. Experiment and discover what works for you. Any structure that clarifies your preferred future and moves you into action is fine.

Distinguish between wanting *and* wanting to want

As you fine-tune your goals, you'll find many that you absolutely want to achieve and some that you really don't intend to achieve, even though you enjoy talking about them.

This tendency is common. Some people get as much pleasure—or even more pleasure—from talking about an upcoming vacation than in actually taking the vacation. Others have great fun talking about the possibility of a sexual adventure that they never intend to have; they just *want to want* the adventure. Some people like to talk about changing jobs; what they really want is the freedom to *talk* about changing jobs.

You can distinguish between wanting to want something and actually wanting it. Notice your behavior over time. If you repeatedly say that you want something yet take no action to get it, then perhaps you just want to want it. This is a great discovery to make. You can forget about the energy, effort, time, and money needed to actually *get* what you say you want. You can make peace with the fact that you will not actually get it. You can just allow yourself to want it, perhaps for many years, until you either stop wanting it or actually take action to get it. Or you can just continue to want it for the rest of your life.

Sometimes it really is okay just to want something and not turn it into a goal that you intend to meet. When you realize this, you can stop criticizing yourself for not getting what you say you want. You can just enjoy the wanting without having to act on your desire.

Turn but to and

"I want to take six months off, but I don't have enough money." "I'd like to change careers, but there's just not enough time in the day to even think about doing that." "I want to buy a house, but I don't want to drain my nest egg for a down payment."

As you envision the life of your dreams, you might find the word *but* creeping into your speaking and writing like an uninvited guest. That small word can produce huge obstacles to creating the future.

There is an alternative: Turn *but* into *and*. When you encounter an obstacle to what you want, turn it into part of your goal: "I will take six months off and have money to spare." "I will continue my life's essential activities and find time to change careers." "I will buy a house and maintain my nest egg." You can then transform these obstacles into action plans. Objections can become part of the package called the life of your dreams.

Reconsider the words be able to

When writing goals, consider deleting the words *be able to*. Thus, the goal "Be able to swim faster" can become "Swim faster." "Be able to love more fully" can become "Love more fully." You probably don't want the ability to do these things—

you just want to *do* them. The words *be able to* can keep you at one remove from achieving your goal.

But at times you may just want a particular ability, hoping that you'll never have to put it to use. For example, you might want physical training that will enable you to defend yourself from a mugger—while hoping that you'll never have to do this. Or you might want such vibrant health that you'll be able to survive a terrible case of the flu—while hoping that you'll never get that sick. The suggestion to reconsider the words *be able to* is just that—a suggestion, not a rule.

Write measurable goals

If you choose goals with results you can measure, you're more likely to meet the goal—and know when you miss it. Instead of stating "Exercise more," you can state "Walk briskly from 7 P.M. to 8 P.M., five days per week." Adding numbers and other specifics increases the chance of achieving success and provides a way to measure progress.

Keep in mind that some of your most worthwhile and important goals can't be measured. For example, you'd be hard pressed to come up with an effective measurement for these: "I will be more spontaneous." "I want to accept people who have ideas that are much different than mine."

State goals positively

Positively stated goals are often more concise and inviting than those stated negatively. Negative goals make clear what you are giving up. Positive goals point out the benefits you stand to gain.

Instead of writing "I will not fall asleep while reading," you can state that goal positively: "I will stay awake when I read." Instead of "I will stop smoking," you can write "I will lead a smoke-free life, I will have clean lungs that are free from nicotine, and I will be tobacco-free." Instead of "I will not overeat," you can write, "I will eat an optimum amount of food for my body" or "I will eat enough food to supply adequate energy and keep myself at my ideal body weight."

Set challenging, achievable goals

If the goals that we take on as promises are too large, then we could become overwhelmed and resign ourselves to never getting what we want. On the other hand, if we set goals that are too small or too easy to achieve, we can get bored.

Review your goals to see if some are so large that they've become a burden. You could eliminate these goals, scale them back, or give yourself more time to achieve them. An advantage of assigning longer time lines to large goals is that you can then break up these goals into smaller tasks. Then what seems unrealistic at first can become a series of challenging yet achievable steps. If you choose to keep a goal that seems burdensome, you can fine-tune it so that it becomes more manageable.

If President Kennedy had called for a moon landing in one year instead of ten, the goal would not have been a challenge to scientists and engineers—it would have been an impossibility. If Nelson Mandela had expected an immediate end to apartheid, South Africans might still be living under that system today. These people and many others like them who called for sweeping changes knew that their goals could take decades to meet.

Change your mind

For some people, the process of writing seems to set a goal in stone. If this is true for you, think of each goal as part of a "first edition" or rough draft of your future. You could also add a paragraph describing the changes you intend to make in the next draft.

There is no final draft of your future. You can even include a statement in your plan to take account of this: "I plan to change this hundred-year plan every year." Your plan is a living document, as flexible and dynamic as life itself. You can revise your goals as often as you want. To make the most of creating your future, revise goals thoughtfully. Living life according to a clear vision lets you make moment-to-moment choices wisely.

WRITE GOALS IN THREE DOMAINS

People often produce most of their goals in the domain of *having*. These goals concern circumstances and things we'd like to have: Have more money, have a three-bedroom house, have a college degree in engineering, have more time.

Having represents only one possible domain. A second domain is action—*doing*. Examples of such goals include "Exercise three times per week," "Attend graduate school," "Travel to Europe," and "Write one hundred words per day in my journal." *Exercise, attend, travel,* and *write* are all action verbs that describe intentions in the realm of doing.

A third domain points to values—*being*. Possible goals in this domain include "Be more loving," "Be more frugal," and "Be more candid in my speaking."

Many plans focus primarily on results or circumstances—what people want to *have*. When creating your future, also choose what you intend to *do* and who you intend to *be*. After distinguishing the domain of the goal, you can begin to balance the number of goals you put into each area.

Take the time now to review the goals you've generated so far.

Sort them into three domains: those that center mainly on what you want to *have*, those that focus on what you want to *do*, and those that are about who you want to *be*. Look for an approximate balance among these three categories. If you wind up with mostly *having* and *doing* goals, then consider creating more *being* goals. For more ways to expand your goals in the domain of being, see "Define your values and align your actions" in the next chapter.

MOVE FROM EXPECTATION TO CHOICE

Separate the goals you freely *choose* from goals that primarily represent what other people *expect* of you. Some of those expectations might be at odds with what you truly want. If you make that discovery, you have the opportunity to take your future back into your own hands.

I believe that a life of your own choosing is more rewarding than a life that someone else chooses for you. And remember that other people do have goals for you. Chances are that your relatives and friends do. Your manager, supervisor, or clients probably do. So do Madison Avenue, Hollywood, and the marketing directors for scores of companies, both large and small. All these people want to influence what you do, what you are, what you buy, what you eat, what you wear, what you see, what you read, and more. And many of them are armed with plans.

The collective expectations of all these people can easily find their way into the goals you create. Review your goals to discern what others expect of you and what you choose.

Please take a few minutes to do this right now. Reread the goals you've written so far. Ask yourself, "Is this something that I freely choose, or am I writing this goal mainly to gain the approval of others?"

If you spot a goal that exists to satisfy an expectation of others, you have at least three options. One is to simply toss out the goal and forget about it. A second option is to ask whether the expectation points to something that you also want. If it does, you can keep that goal. Third, you can rewrite the goal in a way that is aligned with the future you want. For example, the goal "Earn a medical degree" could change to "Earn a degree in sports physiology."

If you're not sure whether a goal represents someone else's expectation or your own choice, then put it aside for now and come back to it later. Raising this question sets your subconscious mind on a quest for clarity. Give it some time, and trust that your mind will deliver the answer.

ELEMENTS OF EFFECTIVE GOALS

The goals open up possibilities

Not all goals open up possibilities for the future, especially those that merely predict the future based on what's happened in the past. Remember that planning by creation can generate many more options than planning by prediction.

We can also shut down possibilities if we forget to write goals in a variety of categories. A person can forget to set goals for recreation or fun and find herself forgetting to take vacations. Reorganizing goals into new categories from time to time can prevent this oversight. We get to see what's missing from our lives and to create new goals or add new categories that fill in the gaps.

The goals give you focus

Planning has at least two distinct phases. One is to open up lots of possibilities, and the other is to narrow the focus in a constructive way. Trying to achieve too many goals can be counterproductive, leaving us feeling disorganized and scattered. Powerful plans have the advantage of eliminating low-priority tasks so that we can focus on achieving what we want most.

The goals help you persist

As you create your future, notice when you're suddenly drawn to make major changes in your life plan or to abandon long-held goals. Having a life plan keeps you on track in making steady progress toward long-range dreams. Once you've thoughtfully created goals and assigned them time lines and priorities, be careful of abandoning them. Detours could lead to dead ends.

To get the most from creating your future, distinguish bold new directions from momentary whims. You might find it valuable to discuss possible major changes in your life plan with a close friend, family member, personal coach, or support group.

The goals are based on lots of input

Perhaps you've done the exercises in this book that involve setting goals with a group. Then you know firsthand about the power of getting input from other people. You've experienced what another person's nonjudgmental speaking and attentive listening can do. If you're stuck, you might find that others can suggest intriguing possibilities.

Many of us were raised according to the myth of self-sufficiency. We got the idea that successful people pull themselves up by their own bootstraps and get the job done alone. This point of view has many shortcomings when applied to creating the future.

We don't have to isolate ourselves to set goals. Many of our goals relate to other people, and we can benefit by involving them directly.

The goals call you forward

If your plans fizzle, look to see whether your goals are aligned with your passion. Creating a future that fails to inspire your passion is like having a sophisticated rocket with the latest guidance system—and no fuel. Experiment with new goals, or rewrite current goals in a way that sparks your enthusiasm.

The energy and excitement generated by creating the future can help you eliminate procrastination from your life. Having a detailed vision of your chosen career can make it easier to handle the next job interview. Knowing that your first novel is due to the publisher in six months can give you the energy to write today.

The goals respond to changes in circumstance

Perhaps you've had the experience of traveling toward a destination, only to encounter a barrier along the way—a surprise thunderstorm, a detour in the road, a flight that's delayed. At these times, reality demands that you make an adjustment in your plan.

The fact that a vision of the future changes from time to time does not detract from its power. It makes sense to change your goals as your circumstances change and as your experience and wisdom grow.

The goals generate multiple pathways to achievement

There's no single, sure-fire recipe for achieving a goal. Knowing this can give you a sense of freedom and mastery. A skilled taxi driver knows several alternative routes to a city's major destinations. A master chef improvises when he cooks, sometimes altering the ingredients and adding new steps to the recipe. A virtuoso jazz musician improvises, playing the same song differently every night.

We can take the same approach to creating the future, reminding ourselves that there are many ways to meet any goal. This is especially true for large or complex goals. For example, we could end world hunger through several different paths: inventing new technology for producing and distributing food, providing economic assistance to poor women, or changing economic policy through new trade agreements. These are just a few of the pathways.

Perhaps you're fond of recipes and step-by-step instructions, and you want to approach your vision of the future in the same way. No problem. Just create at least five different routes to each goal. If you are fond of checklists, then create five different checklists for reaching any goal. The path you eventually choose might be a combination of all five—or something completely different.

The goals can be fine-tuned through action

Taking action is a powerful way of getting feedback on a goal. If your goal makes sense, then putting it into action will probably lead to the results you want. If you left out a step or forgot to consider a major obstacle, taking action will make this clear.

Plans that look good on paper may not hold up on the street. The results you get from taking action often suggest alternative paths toward the goal or ways to refine it. Even if your plan is sketchy, taking it for a test drive will help you arrive at more precise, attainable goals.

Step 4: Carry Out

*How different our lives are when we really know
what is deeply important to us, and, keeping
that picture in mind, we manage ourselves each day
to be and do what really matters most.*

—Stephen R. Covey

MOVE FROM REFLECTION TO ACTION

As you complete the exercises in this book, you will create dozens, hundreds, or even thousands of goals. At that point you might wonder how to turn those goals into reality while staying relaxed and happy.

The twenty-two strategies included here can close the gap between what you want in life and what you have, between what you plan and what you do, between your vision of the kind of person you'd like to become and who you actually are. Below are brief summaries of each strategy, followed by more thorough descriptions.

1. **Survey your life**. When you tell the truth about your effectiveness in many areas, you unleash a force for change.
2. **Practice acceptance**. One way to solve a problem is to begin by loving it.
3. **Examine moment-to-moment choices**. Remembering that genius is in the details, you can treat small choices with care and watch your whole life start to change.
4. **Investigate your role.** In any situation, you can ask, "How have I created this?" and "How can I turn this around?" As a

tool for discovering choices, you can use the "ladder of powerful speaking."

5. **Focus your attention.** Learning to "be here now" releases
   mental distractions and increases your effectiveness at any activity.

6. **Manage your interpretations.** The ways you choose to interpret your circumstances could instantly bring you closer to
   the life of your dreams.

7. **Speak candidly.** When you express yourself fully, you can
   make a loving contribution to yourself and others.

8. **Make and keep promises.** By making promises to yourself
   and others, you can re-create your life and move into action.

9. **Surrender and trust.** Sometimes a powerful way to deal with
   people and events is to stop futile attempts to control them.

10. **Persist.** When faced with a problem, you can keep looking
    for answers beyond the first good solution that occurs to you,
    and you can stay in action until you achieve what you want.

11. **Notice your expectations.** When you become aware of ex-
    pectations, you discover a major source of upset—and ways
    to create happiness.

12. **Listen fully.** Listening can be a whole way of life, an activity
    that affects everything you do.

13. **Enjoy yourself and celebrate.** In almost any situation, even
    the most difficult, you can find a source of delight.

14. **Detach and play full out.** You can fully involve yourself in
    the people and projects in your life, even as you stay loose
    and lighthearted.

15. **Choose your conversations and your community.** To fulfill
    your goals, take part in conversations and associate with peo-
    ple aligned with your purpose, plans, and values.

16. **Revise your habits.** You can improve your life quickly when
    you see faults as habits instead of personal defects.

17. **Appreciate mistakes.** When you know ways to learn from them, mistakes can be powerful teachers.

18. **Think clearly.** Rather than go through your daily routine on automatic pilot, you can be thoughtful and use simple techniques of logic to move directly toward the life of your dreams.

19. **Act courageously.** Fears need not stop you from doing what you've chosen to do.

20. **Manage your associations.** When you link a desired new behavior to pleasure, you can establish it with a minimum of struggle.

21. **Contribute.** Assisting others to get what they want and taking on bigger problems are ways to create a wonderful life for yourself.

22. **Define your values and align your actions.** Personal effectiveness includes being clear about your fundamental values and making choices consistent with them.

Remember that these strategies are never totally perfected by anyone. They represent habits that you can practice for the rest of your life—in some cases, during every hour of the day.

As you read about these strategies, keep three questions in mind:

* How can I use this strategy?
* What can I do differently?
* How will I be different?

Answering these questions can greatly increase the value you get from this chapter.

1. SURVEY YOUR LIFE

Tell the truth about your effectiveness in every area. When you're honest about which aspects of your life are working well— and which are not—you're poised for growth. If you're out of touch with the truth, you might ignore pressing problems, overlook valuable assets, or come up with bogus solutions.

Alcoholics Anonymous offers one of the most popular and successful programs for personal change, and it begins with telling the truth. The first thing AA members do is "tell it like it really is." Step 1 of the AA program offers a timeless example: "We admitted that we were powerless over alcohol, that our lives had become unmanageable."

AA is just one example. People who join Weight Watchers begin by telling the truth about how much they weigh—a ritual that's repeated at the beginning of every meeting. Counselors begin by assessing their clients. Physicians start with careful diagnoses. Coaches size up their team's current abilities. Supervisors, managers, and teachers do the same.

Many of us approach a frank evaluation of ourselves with the same enthusiasm we'd feel for an IRS audit. The word *evaluation* is often associated with negative experiences such as essay tests, job interviews, or performance reviews.

There is another way to think about evaluations. You could see them as chances to solve problems and take charge of your life. You could welcome them as gifts. If evaluations led to more happiness, you might even greet them with excitement.

During evaluations, you might find it natural to judge your shortcomings and feel bad about them. Some people believe that such feelings are necessary to correct their errors.

You can make a different choice. You can discover a way to

gain skill without feeling rotten about how you've performed in the past. You can change the way things are without being upset about the way things have been.

The point is simple: You can love yourself and still work like mad to change yourself. That's a major benefit of surveying your life.

Surveying your life delivers an added benefit: You become a model for others. After watching you, your family, friends, and coworkers might see the power in this strategy and use it to solve long-standing problems.

Telling the truth works for any problem. Talking straight about yourself enhances all other strategies in this book. When you tell the truth about many different aspects of your life, you unleash a tremendous force for change.

2. PRACTICE ACCEPTANCE

You have a ticket to paradise. You hold that ticket right now, and you can use it any time. And every time you use that ticket, you get a free replacement—one you can redeem anywhere, whenever you want.

That ticket is not a real ticket that you actually hold in your hands. It's one you hold in your head. This ticket to paradise is an attitude, a way of thinking, a way of relating to the world. Practice permitting things to be the way they are—right now, in all their hairy imperfection and glorious messiness.

When you are willing to accept your problems, you drain them of much of their negative energy. Once you love a problem—which means telling the truth about it and accepting it for what it is right now—what to do about it often becomes clear. For example, if you learn that the fan belt on your car is broken, you know what to do: Replace it. If your doctor tells you that your cholesterol level is 300, you also know what to do: Alter your diet and exercise patterns.

We could take other approaches to problems like these. Instead of replacing the fan belt, we could complain about the current state of fan belt technology. Instead of exercising, we could blame our high cholesterol on bad heredity.

Another option is simply to change the belt, start exercising, and get on with our lives. Telling the truth and accepting a situation can lead to useful action. Resisting the truth and complaining about it lead nowhere.

Practicing acceptance is about turning our requirements into preferences. It's about noticing what *is* instead of what *should be*. And it's a path you can start today. Every step on the path involves the same process. Simply accept whatever is happening in the present moment.

When people first hear about this strategy, they often think it means to be resigned to the problem—to "just get used to it." Accepting a problem does not have to stop you from acting. One way to start solving problems is to quit resisting them. Fully accepting and admitting the problem allow you to take effective action—perhaps to even free yourself of the problem once and for all.

3. EXAMINE MOMENT-TO-MOMENT CHOICES

Life hinges on the little things. Friendships are developed one small interaction at a time. Books are written word by word, sentence by sentence. A mansion is built board by board, brick by brick. A massive garden begins with a single flower. A hundred-mile hike begins with one step. Corporate dynasties are built one action at a time.

Maybe one shortcoming of so many self-improvement schemes is that they concentrate on huge goals such as happiness, health, love, and wealth. These schemes can bypass the little things: how we sweep the floor, how we shut the door when leaving the house, the way we set down a bag of groceries on the kitchen counter, the way we hold our facial muscles when listening to another person. In examining such moment-to-moment choices, we discover that genius is in the details.

Major choices—such as whom to marry or what career to pursue—make a huge difference in the quality of our lives. But this fact can lead to an inaccurate conclusion about what is important. Rarely do we have an opportunity to make big choices. Yet in every moment we can make small choices that eventually lead to big results.

The way we breathe when feeling stressed, the words we choose to describe a problem, the gestures we make when speaking to a lover—all of these are small things. Seldom are we aware of them. We may not even realize that we're making these choices each moment. Yet all those micro-choices, added together, become a force that determines what we have, do, and become. The way we live the next moment is in fact the way we live our lives.

A big part of examining moment-to-moment choice is noticing process—your habits, the way you usually get things done. Each day you can take some time to step back and watch yourself as an outside observer would. You can see your life as a film being projected on a screen and place yourself in the audience.

Seeing your habits and overall patterns of behavior leads to an insight. If you change one small part of a pattern, the other parts are likely to change also. When you solve small problems, you could be solving large ones at the same time.

For example, if you want to take better care of your overall health, then start by flossing your teeth daily. If you want to become a better listener, then just listen with full attention to the next person you meet. If you want to eat less, start by just skipping a second helping at your next meal. Then reap the benefits in everything you do.

Strategies are a matter of minute-to-minute choices—choices that you're already making. Each choice, no matter how small, can take you on a detour from your goals—or closer to the life of your dreams. You can make those moment-to-moment choices thoughtfully and in line with your purpose. In small steps, you can take transformational leaps that increase your satisfaction and joy.

4. INVESTIGATE YOUR ROLE

Get ready for one of the most unusual suggestions in this book.

Here it is: Our lives work most effectively when we take total responsibility—for everything.

You can take responsibility for lazy, incompetent supervisors.

You can take responsibility for neighbors who consistently play their CDs at a volume that could shatter glass.

You can take responsibility for dogs that howl from midnight until 2:00 A.M.

Whenever you're tempted to blame someone or something, you can do the opposite. You can take responsibility for it. All of it.

Check your first reactions to this suggestion. Perhaps they

went something like this: "No way! This idea is crazy. I will not take the blame for my insensitive neighbor, or for that obnoxious dog, or for that boss who's so incompetent he can barely find his office. If I start taking on things like this, pretty soon you'll ask me to start taking responsibility for poverty, war, and world hunger also."

The first thing you can do to explore this idea is to lighten up. Take this strategy as a point of departure, a suggestive line of thinking. Play with it and see where it leads. For now, do not worry about proving or disproving it.

Taking responsibility is not the same as saying, "Oh, I see, it's my fault." When you hear the word *responsibility*, translate it into *response-ability*. Responsibility is about the ability to respond.

This strategy does not imply that we chose to have rude neighbors or bad bosses. You are not solely responsible for all the circumstances of your life (though it's sometimes interesting and instructive to pretend that you are). Investigating your role means choosing your *response* to any person or circumstance in your life — taking an active rather than passive role and being aware of how you help shape every situation.

You can apply this strategy to almost any problem, large or small. Once I was out on a picnic with my daughter, and she made us cheese sandwiches by cutting slices from a block of cheese. While eating her sandwich, she started complaining about the thickness of the cheese slices, saying, "Boy, this cheese is too thick!" Immediately she saw the humor in her statement. As we laughed, we commented on how often in life we forget that we are the ones who "sliced the cheese." Few of the problems in our lives come uninvited. In many cases, we make the choices that set those problems in motion.

As we take more responsibility for the quality of our lives, we can ask two questions: "What did I do to create this situation? What can I do to turn this situation around?"

Take a man whose marriage is heading for divorce. When asked what's wrong, his answers are all about what *she* did to create his problems: "She doesn't attend to my needs. She wants all the attention. She spends money without telling me."

These complaints sound reasonable. Yet his way of thinking instantly turns the man into a victim. Instead, he can investigate his role in the breakdown by asking what *he* did to create the situation. After looking more deeply, this man might uncover some choices he made that affected his marriage. For example, he might discover that he seldom asks for attention. He might also see that when his wife asks about money, he usually says, "I'm very busy right now. Don't bother me."

The second question is pure magic — "What can I do to turn this situation around?" It refocuses attention. By choosing what we will do next, we stop being a victim and start taking control of life.

The man whose marriage is in trouble could speak clearly about what he wants. He could become an equal partner in making money decisions. By taking simple steps that are entirely within his control, he could help turn his marriage around.

This strategy suggests that happiness might be less about having the right conditions in our lives and more about working with whatever conditions exist. No matter what the circumstance, we can choose where to focus our attention and what to do next.

Climb the "ladder of powerful speaking"

As a tool for investigating your role, you can use an imaginary "ladder of powerful speaking." On this ladder are six rungs, and each rung has a different name: *obligation, possibility, preference, passion, plan,* and *promise.* Each rung represents a certain level of speaking, a certain way of viewing the world.

At any moment, you "stand" on one of these rungs. That is, your speaking exists on one of these levels. Moving up the ladder—speaking less in terms of obligation and more in terms of promise —is one way to increase your personal effectiveness.

More details about each rung on the ladder of powerful speaking follow.

Listen for obligation

Obligation is the bottom rung of the ladder. When people use the following terms, they're probably speaking out of a sense of obligation: *I should, I have to, I must, someone had better, they made me, someone should, I had to, I couldn't help it, I ought to.* On this rung there's little freedom or opportunity to create the future. People who speak this way often perceive themselves as victims of their circumstances.

Speak about possibilities

The next step up the ladder of powerful speaking is *possibility.* When you use phrases such as *I might, I'll consider, I could, maybe I will,* or *I hope,* you make a small but significant step out of the mud of obligation.

Opening up possibilities is far more energizing and exciting than feeling obligated. Obligation puts other people or external circumstances in charge of our lives. Possibility, like all the rungs above it, puts you back in charge. When you speak at this level, you can open up new goals and achieve new results in your life.

Although possibility is more freeing than obligation, some cautions are appropriate. First, we can be careful not to fill up our speaking, and therefore our lives, only with possibilities. A person who is always talking about what he might accomplish someday may never get around to actually doing anything.

The second caution concerns hope. Many wonderful and inspiring stories revolve around people's hopes and dreams. However, when hope takes the place of planning, promising, and action—higher rungs on the ladder of powerful speaking—it can be a deceptive narcotic.

Speak about preferences

I *prefer to* and I *want to* are common expressions at the next level of speaking—preference. It is natural to move from declaring a goal as possible to declaring a clear preference for doing it.

Again, we can be cautious about overusing this rung of the ladder. People might constantly say that they prefer to do something but never get around to doing it.

Speak about passions

This rung of the ladder is about energy. At this level, your words have more punch and your speaking is more animated. When people hear passion in your voice, they realize that you're enthusiastic about a goal you've created; using the words *I'd love to, I'm excited about,* and *I can't wait to* signals passion. When you feel passionate about a goal, you're more likely to take action to achieve it.

There is a catch: Enthusiasm is no substitute for action. Not much is likely to happen until we translate our energy into plans and promises, the next rungs on the ladder.

Speak about plans

You can bring your passion one step closer to reality by speaking about a *plan.* A plan, especially if it is written, helps ensure that you'll back up your passions with action. A plan gives purpose and direction to your passions. Effective plans lay out the specific steps you'll take to achieve a goal.

Speak about your promises

To reach the top of the ladder, you can make a *promise*. Absolute commitment to a goal is shown in phrases such as *I will, I do, I promise to*. Promises are plans backed by ironclad commitment. Promising can help you unleash your potential and free you from self-imposed barriers.

Most of us do not take advantage of the power of promise. We are capable of far more than we've ever imagined, and promises can break through the artificial barriers we've erected to limit our participation in the world. One path to a rich, rewarding life is to make promises that stretch us toward achieving meaningful goals in all areas of life.

Choose your rung

Whenever you speak, you have the option of moving up the ladder of powerful speaking all the way to the level of promising. Also, it's perfectly okay to not move up the ladder. It would be foolish to promise to achieve every goal that you create. As you listen to yourself speak about the future, you can pay attention to which rung of the ladder you're "standing" on. Then you can choose to move up the ladder whenever it makes sense.

5. FOCUS YOUR ATTENTION

You've seen those late night ads for fantastic gizmos that slice, dice, grind, chop, blend, and do everything except change the oil in your car. Often these ads tout a skill, product, or service that promises to transform the quality of your life—all for just $19.95 and a handful of handling charges.

Imagine that what you're reading now is an ad that tells the truth—an ad for a strategy that really *could* transform your life. Also imagine that learning this skill is inexpensive—in fact, free. Then imagine that it's a skill you already have and always have had, though it is not yet fully developed.

Well, this ability is already yours. And it's a skill that you can develop without paying postage or C.O.D. charges. This too-good-to-be-true offer is about the ability to pay attention.

Anything you do will benefit when you pay full attention to it. When you take a walk, you could just take a walk. You would not worry about making the rent or mortgage payment, about buying your child's next pair of shoes, or about those unfinished projects at work. When you eat your favorite food—say, pizza—you could pour all of your attention into the mouth-watering aroma of hot cheese, rich tomato sauce, and freshly baked bread. You wouldn't be thinking about adding transmission fluid to your car or about that cutting remark your boss made last week. You'd just eat pizza, savoring every bite as if it's the first.

In short, you could really show up for life. You could be where you are when you're there. You could do what you're doing when you're doing it. You could "be here now" and melt into the fullness and completeness and happiness of the present moment. You might notice that whenever this happens—for example, while you're fishing, lying on the beach, or staring at a sunset— you tend to feel fulfilled and complete.

Like most other great ideas, this one is simple and extraordinary at the same time. It's marvelous because you can use it at any time and any place. This strategy is available to you every second that you're awake.

Consider this: Every aspect of your life right now—your job, your relationships, your possessions—flow from where you place your attention. You take action to gain these things, and taking any action calls for focused attention. Perhaps the overall quality of your life simply reflects the way in which you choose to focus your attention.

When you first begin to take note of your attention, you may discover that it is hardly ever "here." Even after years of practice, a person's attention may still frequently wander. Knowing that this will occur, you can lighten up and forgive yourself at those times when your mind seems to have a mind of its own. Gently refocus your attention again . . . and again . . . and again . . . it will boost the power and quality of everything you do.

6. MANAGE YOUR INTERPRETATIONS

Often we think that achieving the life of our dreams involves having everything we'd love to have and doing everything we'd love to do—that the life of our dreams depends entirely on having ideal circumstances. Although I believe that's a practical approach, it is incomplete. Satisfaction could have as much, or even more, to do with the way we interpret our circumstances as with our success at creating the circumstances we want. Managing the way we think about our experience can dramatically increase our happiness without our making the slightest change in circumstances.

Separate facts from interpretations

To understand how this strategy works, remember the difference between facts and interpretations. Many people operate as if *facts* and their *interpretations of the facts* and are one and the same thing. They observe a fact, make up an interpretation or a story about it, and then act as if the interpretation is a fact.

For example, ask someone to state a fact about a person whom he dislikes. He may say, "Well, he's rude." This statement is actually an interpretation. If you press for details, you might eventually run across a verifiable observation—a fact: "He walked right by me and didn't say hello." But saying that he's rude is only one of many possible interpretations. Perhaps he was deep in thought and didn't notice anyone around him. Perhaps he was rushing to a meeting that had started ten minutes earlier and wasn't paying attention.

Consider another example. A woman walks into your office and starts screaming, telling you how upset she is with you. After observing this, many people would take it as a fact that this woman has little respect for you. However, you could consider other interpretations. For instance, you could say that this woman does generally respect you and is highly committed to making your relationship work—so committed that she brought the conflict out in the open, although somewhat ungracefully, so that it could be resolved.

Choose useful interpretations

There are a variety of ways to interpret almost anything you observe. Knowing this, you can re-create your world at any moment. Just choose another interpretation about what you see, hear, or feel. This choice can transform your life.

I've noticed interpretations at work in my relationship with my wife, Trisha. Most of the time when I come home from work, she greets me with a smile and a warm hug. When that happens, I find it easy to accept the interpretation that she loves me very much and is thrilled with our relationship.

On rare occasions, however, Trisha will wrinkle her forehead and just greet me in passing. At those times I can start to manufacture all kinds of interpretations: She had a hard day at work. She's feeling ill. She's upset with me. She no longer cares as much about me as I do about her. Sometimes I consider the interpretation that the deep love and intimacy we've enjoyed have disappeared.

The interpretation I choose will make a big difference in what I say and do next. If I conclude that she probably doesn't care about me anymore, then I might respond with a question that comes across like an accusation: "What's *your* problem with me *today?*"

Instead, I could look for other possible interpretations. I could remember that she normally greets me affectionately. I can keep my interpretation that she loves me very much and is totally committed to our relationship. Now it's easier for me to consider the possibility that something else is on her mind. I can listen to her without judgment, find out what's going on, and deal with it appropriately.

This more useful interpretation encourages appropriate behavior. I can simply share the facts—what I see, hear, and feel—and use them as a basis for communicating: "I notice that you've spoken to me very little since I got home and I'm wondering what's on your mind." That's a lot easier for Trisha to hear than sarcasm: "You're sure being cold to me. What's *your* problem?" By increasing my repertoire of interpretations, I immediately increase my repertoire of behaviors.

To create the kind of loving relationship I want, I do not have to change anything about my circumstances. I don't need to buy a new house, get a new job, or marry someone else. Changing my experience of Trisha is just a matter of choosing a useful interpretation that's aligned with my goals and commitments for the future, which include a long and loving relationship with Trisha.

Remember four cautions

As you practice managing your interpretations, keep four helpful points in mind.

First, I'm not saying that interpretation should be eliminated. We need interpretations in order to make sense of the world. But at any time you are free to distinguish interpretations from facts, choose useful interpretations, and then act on those interpretations.

Second, be careful to choose interpretations that are both useful and accurate. We might be tempted to accept interpretations that seem useful because they get us off the hook, let us take the path of least resistance, or allow us to continue believing something we desperately want to believe. If those interpretations deny relevant facts, we are setting ourselves up for problems.

For example, some parents believe that their children can do no wrong. When their children misbehave, these parents find an interpretation that shelters the children from the natural consequences of their behavior. Having faith in children is wonderful. When this attribute includes distorting the facts, children are robbed of the opportunity to learn.

A third caution is to avoid using this strategy as a substitute for appropriate action. A person in an abusive relationship can create dozens of ways to interpret that circumstance. In addition, she could improve the quality of her life and possibly save the relationship by leaving for a while and getting professional help.

Finally, be careful of the need to find the "right" interpretation. I'm not sure we can ever know the most truthful or accurate interpretation of any circumstance. What we can do is consider a variety of interpretations and choose those that are both accurate and useful and that will lead to the life of our dreams.

7. SPEAK CANDIDLY

Most of us can remember a situation in which we kept quiet when we should have said something.

Maybe you were angry when someone insulted you, but you felt frightened and didn't respond.

Maybe you came up with an idea that would have solved a problem, but you felt embarrassed and didn't share it.

Or maybe the timing was perfect for the hilarious comment you had in mind, but you were too self-conscious to say anything.

Being frightened, embarrassed, or self-conscious can keep us from speaking candidly. When we hold back, we cheat ourselves and the people we love.

Our speaking can provide helpful feedback for others. Instead of using words to cut people down, we can help people experience success. Feedback is just a tool. Like any other tool, it can be used to harm or to help. Feedback can be given with ill will or with love.

Refusing to speak our minds can cheat others of a chance to look at a problem from a new angle. Remember that others can choose how to respond to what we say. If they choose to ignore our ideas, we've still communicated the fact that we care. And if they use our ideas to make a positive change, everyone wins.

Consider the woman who feels hurt every time her partner talks about his past relationships. Her partner genuinely loves her and would stop these comments if he knew the effect they had on her. By keeping her feelings to herself, she denies her partner the opportunity to change his behavior, and she might find herself lashing out about insignificant issues. If she chose to reveal what she's really thinking and feeling, the couple could solve this problem. More often than not, truthful speaking is useful speaking.

One way to clarify your message and avoid hurting others is to tell people what you are *not* saying: "I want more time alone. I am not saying that I want to end our relationship." "I wish you would stop playing it so safe. I am not saying that you should take foolish risks or needless chances." Adding this dimension to your speaking can prevent people from filling in the gaps with faulty assumptions of their own.

No suggestion is absolute, including the suggestion to speak candidly. There are times when it is appropriate and effective to not speak. These are times when our speaking could hurt someone, spoil the punch line, or rob others of the opportunity to learn from their own experience.

Although it might be useful to monitor what we say, most of us err on the side of playing it too safe. One powerful way to take better care of ourselves and others is to speak more, not less.

Talking about your feelings, whatever they are, is a path toward releasing them and healing relationships. After expressing a tough emotion like anger, you could find out that there's compassion underneath it. Saying "I'm so angry at you for staying away so long" can lead to "I missed you" or even "I love you."

So, don't rehearse. Don't wait for the right moment. Don't worry if the syntax is right. Don't weigh your words. Don't worry about how it will sound or if people will still like you. Just say it, and ask others to do the same.

8. MAKE AND KEEP PROMISES

Giving your word is a powerful step in creating a compelling future. When you make a promise, your word is almost as good as the action itself.

Life works to the degree that we keep our promises. Often, when something goes wrong in the world or in our lives, the problem goes back to a broken agreement.

Imagine how different life would be if all promises were kept. Marriage vows would be honored. Loans would be paid off when they were due. Treaties between nations would be respected. When our words and our behaviors are aligned, we often experience a sense of comfort, control, and freedom.

The ability to make and keep promises is a skill that can be learned. Here are a few strategies that can help.

Make challenging yet realistic promises

Effective promises invite us to meet our potential. At the same time, they represent results we can actually achieve. If our promises are too audacious ("I'll become a world-class athlete in six months"), we set ourselves up for failure. If they are too easy ("I promise to get up tomorrow morning"), we insult ourselves. Realistic promises are possible to accomplish and also involve stretching ourselves to meet them.

We can also forgive ourselves when we break a promise. When we're out to maximize our potential and discover our limits, we'll probably break promises once in a while.

Examine consequences

The consequences of keeping or breaking promises vary. Promising to go to a movie tonight is different than promising to pay taxes on time. The stakes become higher when we sign legal documents or when we declare marriage vows. Knowing the consequences of breaking or having to renegotiate a promise can help us choose whether or not to make it in the first place.

When appropriate, negotiate changes

Negotiating a change in a promise can be useful when you are still willing to fulfill it. If you see an alternative that might offer an improvement or if a different time line would be more convenient, you can request a renegotiation. You can point out that you are still willing to keep the original promise and wish to make a modification. In some cases, you can even go as far as to ask to be released from the promise. If you are no longer willing or able to keep it, renegotiating is irrelevant. It's time to revoke the promise.

Ask other people to hold you accountable

Many of us are more likely to keep promises made to other people than promises made only to ourselves. This points to a powerful strategy that can help us keep our promises. We can choose people we trust, ask them to accept our promises, and request that they hold us accountable.

For example, you could ask key people in your life to accept your promise to exercise three times this week. These people can check on you periodically, and you can report to them on progress or let them know when the promise has been completely fulfilled.

Keep promises visible

There's probably some truth to the old saying "Out of sight, out of mind." Keeping visual reminders of your promises can help you keep your word. You can create many ways to display promises. For example, write them on 3×5 cards taped to your desk, or write them in calligraphy to be framed.

Design a detailed action plan

One way to reach a goal or fulfill a promise is to break it down into smaller steps. You can often divide a large goal into smaller actions that can be completed in one hour or less.

Report breakdowns early

When you become aware of potential barriers to keeping a promise, you can report these barriers early on. This gives you and others time to adjust and to create strategies to help you keep the promise.

Early reports also minimize the chances of unwelcome surprises: "What do you mean, you'll need another two weeks for that report?" "I thought you were planning to pick me up at five o'clock, not six." "Aren't you taking care of the kids tonight, as we planned?" "Why didn't you tell me?"

Get help

You can involve other people in fulfilling your promise. Perhaps they could suggest solutions or actually take over some tasks. Take advantage of all possible resources in order to fulfill your promises.

Create a promise-making ceremony

You can invite friends and relatives to a formal ceremony during which you declare your promises. Ceremonies are already commonly used to celebrate a wide variety of promises— treaty signings, confirmations, and bar mitzvahs. When rituals, ceremonies, and official public declarations accompany your promises, you are more likely to keep them.

9. SURRENDER AND TRUST

This book is in large part about taking charge of your life. It's about taking responsibility for your choices—to stop being the victim and start being the victor, no matter what life tosses your way.

With that in mind, you might think it illogical for me to include a strategy in this book about surrendering. That's right. It is illogical. But after all, life is larger than logic.

At times it pays to step out of the way and give up control. We can quit fighting what's happening. We can start riding the horse in the direction it's already going.

At times life backs us into a corner and brings us to our knees. Almost all of us experience times when all our approaches to solving problems fall flat. At those times it's wise to bend. We can admit we're stumped. We can admit that we'll never make it by ourselves.

There's magic in this admission. Once we admit we're at the end of our rope, we open ourselves to receiving help. We give up thinking that we have to be in control of everything. Basically, we just surrender. And that opens a space for something new in our lives.

There are countless examples of this. A student raises her hand in class and admits that she's totally lost, with no clue as to what the teacher is talking about. Now the teacher can help her frame a meaningful question. An alcoholic admits that he just can't control his drinking. This becomes the key that allows him to seek treatment. A person with multiple sclerosis admits that she's gradually losing her ability to walk and tells others about it. Now the people around her can understand, be supportive, and explore ways to help. In each of these cases, the people involved learned the power of surrendering and asking for help.

It's easy to misunderstand what surrendering is all about. Keep some cautions in mind.

First, surrender does not mean giving up or refusing responsibility. Surrender is simply telling the truth—that you don't always have an ace up your sleeve, that you don't always know the answer.

Second, surrender is not the same as being lazy or avoiding effort. You can surrender and, at the same time, continue to invest lots of time and intense energy in a project. Surrender is not necessarily accompanied by inactivity. Some people surrender to a toothache. That strategy particularly makes sense when they're driving to the dentist's office.

Third, there's power in surrendering even when things are going well. This strategy can be valuable at any time, not just when you're having problems. When you're succeeding, when you're regularly setting and meeting goals, you can acknowledge the help you received from others. You can be thankful for all the gifts that came your way without your asking for them—the caring and concern freely given by family, friends, teachers, mentors, and others. Surrendering can be a posture toward life in general, a lens through which you view each event with limitless gratitude.

If you choose to surrender, then you can also choose to trust. You can trust dawn to follow darkness. You can trust that you will come out on the other side of problems with new strength and wisdom. You can trust the process of change, choosing when to give up control and when to ask for help. You can also remind yourself that help is often available from sources that you might not expect or understand. You can surrender—and win.

10. PERSIST

When looking for a breakthrough in your life, you can take a cue from a humble piece of technology—the old-fashioned water pump. When you first start moving the pump handle, no water comes out of the faucet. You might work for a full minute while you're priming the pump. If you persist, you'll be rewarded with fresh, cold water. But if you give up too soon, any water already in the pipe will flow back into the ground. Even though you'll get some exercise from pumping the handle, you'll walk away dry.

Persistence will also pay off if you ever intend to grow bamboo. Once you plant the bamboo seed, you might not see any growth for years or even decades. But when your plant does bloom, be prepared for a huge reward. Bamboo trees can grow several feet in one day, and they usually reach their full height—as much as 120 feet—in just a few months.

These examples suggest a useful strategy for overcoming obstacles to the life of your dreams: Persist. Continue. Sustain effort. Be patient. Give yourself time to overcome inertia and the pull of old ideas. When you're attempting to solve a problem or reach any goal, the last solution you invent could be the one that works. If you stop creating too soon, you could miss the payoff. Many of us get frustrated and quit just moments before we succeed.

Keep looking for answers

When applied to the realm of problem solving, persistence

means looking for answers. Answers are wonderful, especially when they resolve our most troubling questions and deeply felt concerns. But answers can also get in the way. Once we're convinced that we have *the* answer to a question, it's easy to stop looking for more answers. And if the first answers or solutions we find don't work, then we're stuck with our problems.

Instead of latching on to one answer, you can look for more. Instead of being content with the first or easiest option that comes to mind, you can keep searching. Even when you're convinced that you've finally handled a problem, you can find five more solutions and open up new worlds of possibilities.

When presented with a new idea, many people pride themselves in being critical thinkers. They look for problems. They probe for weaknesses. They constantly play the role of devil's advocate. Their overriding concern is to avoid mistakes at all costs. Their main question seems to be "What's wrong with this idea?"

This approach can be useful at times. However, if it is the *only* tool we use, we can come up short. When we constantly look for what's wrong with new ideas, we can miss what does work.

A different approach is to ask "What if that idea is true?" Rather than look for what's wrong, you can seek what's potentially valuable. Faced with a new idea, you can stay in the inquiry, look deeper, and go farther.

Even if an idea is foolish or unsound, asking "What if that's true?" does no harm. Under the spotlight, unsound ideas have a habit of revealing their true nature. In the meantime, considering even the craziest ideas and acting on them can lead you to unexpected benefits.

Sometimes, looking for new answers involves letting go of familiar, even cherished, ideas. One key to persisting is agreeing to temporarily suspend a belief or an idea that you hold as certain. When you do this, remember that you can reclaim the belief or idea at any time.

Stay in action

Persistence is also important in the realm of action. If you find that it takes a great deal of time to conceive a new idea or to complete the first few steps of a large project, you might start feeling defeated. That's when you can remember the bamboo tree. Perhaps a new outcome for your life is germinating, existing in a state of pure potential. Perhaps you're poised for sudden, dramatic growth. The next action you take could be the one that produces the most visible change.

Countless advances became possible when their creators persisted in both thinking and action. Sigmund Freud asked why people behave irrationally. His persistence led to the fruitful and influential concept of the unconscious mind. A group of electrical engineers asked if they could invent a digital component smaller and more efficient than a transistor. Their persistence led to the computer chip. In these cases and many more, people suspended prevailing beliefs and kept asking questions that might have seemed foolish or unrealistic at the time. And they kept taking action until they produced the outcome they desired.

In my work as a coach who helps people create the future and meet their high-priority goals, I heard a client say something that beautifully illustrates the power of persistence: "The biggest threat to an extraordinary life is a good one, not a bad one." That's a powerful way of stating what we often observe. People might find that meeting a few of their goals produces a pretty good life—perhaps not the life of their dreams, but a reasonably satisfying life.

My wish is that you will become creatively discontent. I don't want you to settle for a life that's reasonably satisfying. I want you to have a life that surpasses what you now consider to be your wildest dreams and most audacious goals. I want you to create a vision so enticing that it pulls you into immediate action.

As you read this book and do the exercises, I request that you persist. Avoid settling on the first goals that come to your mind. Persist until you've pushed through any obstacles to your greatness and the future you'd love to have.

11. NOTICE YOUR EXPECTATIONS

Expectations can dominate our thinking, influence our behavior, and seriously get in the way of a wonderful life.

Often expectations take the form of pictures—images of what we want or need in order to be satisfied. The person who wants to be rich doesn't want just a pile of money stashed in a bank vault. She probably has specific mental pictures of what riches can bring to her life: perhaps a new Mercedes loaded with chrome, a twenty-six-room mansion with an Olympic-size swimming pool, a hundred-acre estate lined with tennis courts and lush flower gardens, or the ability to give away lots of money to her favorite charities.

Just about any time we feel a need, we conjure up a picture of what will satisfy that need. This habit starts early. A baby feels hunger pangs and starts to cry. Within seconds, the mother appears and the baby is satisfied. The baby stores a mental picture of herself crying and then getting fed. She connects that picture with stopping the hunger. Now she knows how to solve the hunger problem, and the picture goes on file.

We could even say that our minds function like a huge photo album. Its pages include pictures of all the ways in which we've satisfied needs in the past. And whenever we feel dissatisfied, we mentally search the album for a picture of how to make the dissatisfaction go away. With that picture firmly in mind, we behave in ways that will make the world outside our heads match the picture.

Pictures serve us. In fact, we need them in order to survive. Imagine trying to find your way to work without an accurate mental picture of the streets of your city. The problem is, pictures can also get in our way. Sometimes this happens when the outside world changes, but mental pictures stay the same.

Consider the college student who looks forward to returning home to see his parents at spring break. During the flight home, he pictures his mother and father nestled in the living room by the fireplace as they always do after eating dinner. He calls up a mental picture of his bedroom and sees the exact location of each object in that room—the easy chair, compact disc player, and the stacks of his favorite CDs.

When he finally arrives at the airport, his parents greet him warmly. Then, after some small talk, his father delivers the news: "Son, your mother and I sold the house and most of our belongings. Since we're retired now and you're almost done with school, we've chosen to live the carefree life. We've bought a recreational vehicle big enough to sleep four. Wait until you see it! It's got Naugahyde furnishings, bunk beds, two built-in Porta Pottis, and even an artificial fireplace."

Our student is crushed. Gone is his room and all the resting places for those cherished possessions. He starts making up pictures of his parents' RV. And in his mind he sees a cramped, clanky, gas-guzzling mobile home that smells like burnt oil.

This is just one example of how pictures and reality can conflict—and how negative feelings can result. Any time you feel depressed, anxious, or sad, check to see how reality is violating one of your precious mental pictures. When pictures start to get in your way, there are at least five ways to respond.

One is to just notice your mental pictures. You might find that this option alone is powerful enough to dissolve many upsets. Simply becoming aware of what your pictures are and how they affect you is a huge step to decreasing their power. You might discover that you can have a wonderful life even when the picture, or expectation, keeps going unmet. Once we notice our pictures of wealth, we might be able to feel wealthy even without the mansion ringed with tennis courts.

Sometimes we can let go of old pictures and replace them with new, more realistic ones. That's a second option. Return to our unhappy college student for a minute. He could take a second look at his mental pictures of his old house. When he's willing to tell the truth about that place, he remembers that his room had closet doors that never shut tight. The floorboards creaked mercilessly on winter mornings. What's more, he recalls that the fireplace was pretty but sucked a lot of warmth out of the room.

Then he sees his parents' RV for the first time. He's pleasantly surprised. The trailer is more spacious than he had expected. The furnishings are stylish and modern. The bunk beds are actually comfortable, and the stereo system is a knockout. His old pictures of RVs as bulky, stuffy, and generally dorky just don't match reality.

With this discovery, he creates a new mental picture of family bliss—one that's more in tune with the present reality. He sees himself lounging on a bunk bed, singing along with his parents to their favorite tape as they hit the highways to Malibu.

There is a third option for dealing with mental pictures. When you're fully aware of the unmet expectation or need that is creating a difficulty, you're free to set goals to meet it. Noticing your expectations becomes fuel for creating your future. This option is especially useful when mental pictures have led to actions that satisfy needs but also produce significantly negative consequences. Belonging to a gang is an example. Gangs present one picture of how to satisfy the fundamental need to belong. Membership in a gang also comes with huge costs, which can include injury, incarceration, or even death. Faced with this fact, people can set goals to satisfy the need without the costs — for example, to find belonging in an athletic team, a church group, or a loving family. Sometimes the ability to create new mental pictures can save lives.

A fourth option for dealing with mental pictures is to change them into requests. For instance, if you expect your coworkers to be on time (your mental picture) and they generally aren't, your job could become a source of continual frustration. An alternative is to make an explicit request that your coworkers be more punctual. This gets your expectation out on the table.

A fifth option is to simply let go of more and more pictures. With this option, you don't replace old pictures with new ones. You simply live with fewer pictures and pay more attention to accepting whatever occurs. This option serves your happiness. The fewer pictures you have, the less likely it is that other people and events will violate your expectations. And the chances decrease that you will view people and events with frustration, fear, anger, or sadness.

There's one point behind all of these options for dealing with pictures: We can take charge of the images that float through our minds. We don't have to be ruled by an album of antique pictures — we no longer have to cry for our food. Our pictures can become as fluid and flexible as reality itself.

12. LISTEN FULLY

Most people think listening is what you do when someone else talks. Giving your complete and nonjudgmental attention when others speak is one important, valuable form of listening. However, listening can be much more—a way of life, a total approach to the world. Listening fully is one way to boost your opportunities for happiness, health, love, wealth, or any other goals you choose.

Begin with a larger meaning for the word *listen*. Listening in this sense means receiving *anything*. When you listen to someone talk, you receive their words. When your stereo is playing, you receive music. When you turn on your television, you receive programs. On your birthday, you receive gifts. When you feel a headache and runny nose, you receive a message from your body about a possible oncoming cold. Noticing and responding to each of these events is *listening* in the wider sense of that word.

Listening fully means receiving whatever the world is "sending." At any given moment the world is sending plenty—thousands of tastes, sights, aromas, sounds, textures, bodily sensations, ideas, and bits of information just waiting to be noticed. If we are not careful and conscious, we might inadvertently tune out huge parts of this symphony of sights and sounds.

The American Heritage Dictionary defines the word *listen* this way: "To make a conscious effort to hear; to attend closely; to give heed." This is a useful definition. Listening fully means paying exquisite, close attention.

When you pay attention, your world gets bigger. You can test this idea for yourself. Just put this book down for two minutes. Close your eyes and notice everything you hear at this moment.

Next, open your eyes and notice all the colors you see. Congratulations. You've just entered a new world, larger and far richer in
sights and sounds than the world you inhabited two minutes ago.

When we listen effectively, we receive the messages that
world sends us and are better able to take effective action. Human beings suffer when their actions are at odds with the way the
world works. The musician who constantly plays in a different
key than the rest of the band can get fired. The person who's al-
lergic to dairy products will get sick if she keeps drinking milk-
shakes.

One meaning of happiness is living in tune with the way
things are. This does not mean to just accept the status quo or "go
along with it" in a way that violates our values. Instead, this strategy calls for listening—moment-by-moment attention to the
world inside us and outside us. The better we listen, the better we
can play with the band . . . or choose a new band.

Listening becomes useful when you feel upset and don't
know why. Often something in the background, just beneath the
surface of your attention, is affecting you: the rumbling of an air
conditioner, a pebble in your shoe, or a gut feeling that something about a key relationship in your life is not working. In these
situations you can stop and ask, "What am I not noticing? What
am I forgetting to hear?" Then listen for the answer. A little attention and corrective action can make all the difference.

Listening to ourselves is also a way to detect any difference
between what we say and what we do. Someone who says he's a
good listener might discover that in many conversations he actually does most of the talking. Someone who advises others to be
on time might notice that she often shows up for meetings fifteen
minutes late. Listening to ourselves helps us notice and change
such gaps between our words and deeds, our actions and values.

At times you might notice another kind of gap—a conflict between what you value and the kind of conversations going on around you. Some of those conversations might be about predicting the future instead of creating it. Other conversations might focus on reasons that people missed their goals instead of new strategies for meeting those goals. To practice effective listening, remember that you can choose your conversations. Avoid those that are not useful. And when you choose to listen, listen fully.

13. ENJOY YOURSELF AND CELEBRATE

The motto "No pain, no gain" can easily lead us astray. Consider another point of view: Maximum contribution comes from maximum fun. High productivity comes from high enjoyment. People who celebrate are more likely to excel. And, at any moment, we can take the time to enjoy and celebrate.

Compare two work environments. The employees in one office barely speak to one another. At lunchtime everyone huddles at their desks for solitary sack lunches. By midafternoon these desperate people start watching the clock. They're silently waiting for the time when they can slink out the door, unnoticed. Despite the nose-to-the-grindstone atmosphere that prevails here, the company is barely profitable.

The people who work in the other office see one another regularly. At the beginning of each meeting, they socialize for a few minutes. This practice paves the way for enduring friendships that extend beyond working hours. What's more, their cubicles and hallways occasionally reverberate with the sound of laughter. The prevailing spirit of cooperation and teamwork leads to sustained growth and low employee turnover.

These examples point to an idea you can practice in every

area of your life. In each moment you can find something to enjoy and celebrate.

Remembering this strategy can work wonders as you create goals and take action to achieve them. Many people believe that success calls for ceaseless effort, self-denial, self-discipline, and a little suffering thrown in for good measure. I don't know about you, but I have no interest in suffering as a path to creating my future. Instead, my passion is to have the life of my dreams and to enjoy myself at every step of the way.

I know that this philosophy of success flies in the face of conventional wisdom. But I think that suffering and self-discipline can create a lot of problems. One is that even though we may meet our goals by this route, we can become so unhappy in the process that we just say to heck with it and forget about goals altogether. Another problem is that we could succeed in meeting most or even all our goals—and find that it takes too much suffering and self-discipline to maintain what we achieve. Either way, we create misery.

A classic example of these two problems is the seesaw that people ride in their efforts at weight control. A standard approach to weight control is to adopt a stern program of self-control—forcing yourself to eat less by restricting food portions, skipping desserts, giving up the foods you love, and so on.

These are all examples of self-discipline that entails suffering. People can do this for a while—for six months, maybe even a year. They can even maintain their self-discipline until they lose weight. The problem is that they are skinny but suffering, lighter but not more lighthearted. It's no surprise when they eventually shuck their self-discipline and go back to their old habits of overeating. These people get a taste of self-discipline and conclude that it's not worth it. They just want to enjoy life again.

An alternative to this cycle of suffering and self-indulgence is to take a slower and more satisfying approach to weight control. There are lots of options for doing this. One is to find low-fat, low-calorie foods that you genuinely love and to eat them without guilt. Another is to start some form of exercise that you truly enjoy and to do it with your friends. By taking these steps, you can lose weight while having a ball. You can do something in your best self-interest and make the whole process joyful, easy, and effortless.

This practice of enjoyment and celebration can work even when circumstances become difficult. Shortly before my father died in 1989, he and my mother made a commitment to rejoice during the last months before his impending death. They spoke about this commitment every time I saw them or talked to them on the phone. Their intention was to spend the last days of my dad's life celebrating all the years they'd enjoyed together and the wonderful lives they'd been able to lead. Rejoicing was the theme of my father's funeral, and it was the theme of the last chapter of his life. From his example, I saw that celebration in the midst of difficulties can be more than a nice idea—it can be real and straight from the heart.

While my mother was dying of cancer in 1997, I think she felt that the word *rejoice* was sacred, something reserved for my father's death. Though she didn't use that word, she still brought the same sense of celebration and enjoyment to the end of her life. And it was not a comfortable ending. She grew weak and had difficulty breathing. During her last month, my mother went largely without food and could hardly swallow water.

To my surprise, she started eating a little Jell-O at this time. All my mother's life, she'd refused Jell-O. It was just one of those foods that she never ate and never liked. But in those last days we were able to feed her Jell-O along with a little pudding and some ice chips—her main sources of nutrients.

My mother discovered that she loved peach Jell-O, which her sister made with fresh peaches. According to my daughter Elizabeth, Mother would lie in bed with her eyes closed and open her mouth wide to signal Elizabeth that it was time for another spoonful of Jell-O. After taking each bite, Mother smiled and said, "Mmmmm." She was able to savor that simple food as if it were the finest meal on earth. In those moments, my mother kept her commitment to rejoice—the same commitment she had made eight years earlier with my father.

I am not saying that my mother celebrated every minute of her last days. There were many times when she was visibly upset, clearly grieving the end of her life. Still, she smiled every time I saw her. Each time she found something to celebrate.

Other experiences in my life also taught me about the power of celebration in any circumstance. When I visited Bangladesh in 1994 and India in 1996, I spent time with people who lived in abject poverty. Most of them had little to eat. Often they had no chimney for their indoor fires and no clean water. Most didn't even have toilets indoors or out.

My initial reaction was to feel miserable and sorry for people living in these conditions. Strangely, my feelings quickly turned to a sense of celebration, just as they did when my mother was dying. In part, I celebrated the fact that I wasn't dying and that I wasn't hungry. But there was more. I saw that people who seemed to have nothing often laughed. They took pleasure in the moment, enjoying the simplest and most universal things—their children, their families, their daily tasks—and they were gracious and pleasant hosts. They were often lighthearted and joyous. Against a background of such extreme poverty, I saw these moments as precious. I realized more deeply than ever the sacredness of life.

From my parents' deaths and from the people I saw in India and Bangladesh, I take profound lessons. If my mother in the hours before she died could so fully celebrate peach Jell-O—and if people in abject poverty could enjoy life—then I need a real wake-up call if I ever stop celebrating. Struggle and sorrow are facts, and they can fully coexist with enjoyment and even rejoicing.

14. DETACH AND PLAY FULL OUT

When it comes to managing stress, we can take a cue from a wise, patient, all-knowing, but little-known sage named Russet. Russet has a technique for meeting adversity in life, and it works with almost 100 percent efficiency. When confronted with a distressing situation, Russet just puffs up her cheeks, purses her lips, and blows air out of her mouth with sudden force. It's difficult to duplicate this sound in print—something like *bbbbbbbffffffffff-bbbbbbbffffffth*. This technique works even better when she shakes her head, slobbers, and drools a little bit at the end.

When Russet does this, she sounds just like a horse, which stands to reason: Russet is a horse. Russet's stress management technique has been affectionately named "horse lips."

Lighten up . . .

We can do "horse lips" at any time. This is a great illustration of the power of detachment—finding ways to lighten up and stop taking ourselves so seriously.

Imagine that at a crucial meeting your boss asks you for the answer to a pressing question. The atmosphere is charged with a murderous tension. Your job may hang on how you perform at this single moment. Meanwhile, your body is a mass of knots. Your gut is churning. You have no idea what to say. You're about to despair.

Suddenly you remember Russet, and you know what to do. You pause, wait for the moment of maximum impact, and at just the right time . . . you think, "*bbbbbbbffffffffffffbbbbbbbfffffth!*"

Laughter can restore perspective and renew us. Lightening up can lift us out of a dilemma and help us find new solutions to a problem.

Other statements express this idea: Be lighthearted. Take it easy. Loosen up. Let go. Each saying makes a useful suggestion. They can be summed up in one word: detach.

. . . and stay in the game

Our challenge is to be detached while applying another set of suggestions that are just as useful: Work as if your life depended on it. Live each day as if it will be your last. Get off the sidelines. These ideas can be summed up in one phrase: play full out.

The suggestions to detach and to play full out might seem to contradict each other. They do not. Actually, these two approaches support each other. They are as necessary to each other as night is to day, as breathing out is to breathing in.

If you want to meet your goals, then practice working hard and letting go. Take it seriously and laugh about it all. Change what you can and accept what you cannot change. Go with the flow and make the flow.

The trick is to hold both ideas in balance. We can play life full out and not take it too seriously.

Notice your attachments

Attaining balance is often easier when we take a new view of our roles. Ask someone, "Who are you?" Chances are, he'll respond by listing his roles:

> *"I'm a teacher."*
> *"I'm a supervisor."*
> *"I'm a married man."*
> *"I'm a sports nut."*
> *"I'm a BMW owner."*
> *"I'm a good worker."*

When we link our happiness and well-being to jobs, possessions, looks, and money, we become attached to them. We make our roles more important than our souls. This type of attachment is one of the biggest obstacles to creating a wonderful life. The things we habitually attach ourselves to are fleeting and impermanent, so they're bound to disappoint us. Bodies age. Hair falls out. Joints stiffen. Cars rust, and clothes go out of fashion. Careers change. Fortunes are won, then lost.

There's no harm in roles as long as we keep them in perspective. The problem comes when we let our roles run our lives.

Attachment to roles can take the form of equations inside our heads. For example, when I am attached to my car, it's as if I am living by an equation: DAVE = CAR. Then if I'm in an accident and somebody smashes my car, it's as if they wrecked me. Now, besides having to deal with my broken car, I have to deal with my broken self. An alternative is to notice my attachment to my car and remember that I can be fine even if my car is wrecked. When I remember this fact, I can let go of the equation. Now I have a car; it doesn't have me.

I could also become attached to my money, which leads to another equation: DAVE = MONEY. Then if I lost my money, I might conclude that life would not be worth living. I'm sure this thought occurred to many people when the New York Stock Exchange crashed in 1929 and had another fall in 1987. Some people who had a lot of money invested in the stock market killed themselves because they were so attached to their money. The overriding equation in their heads was I = MY MONEY or I = MY NET WORTH. What we can again do is remember that we are more than our bank accounts. Even if we go bankrupt, we can go on living. Then we can have money; it doesn't have us.

Sometimes the equations behind our attachments hit a little closer to home. For instance, it's more challenging to understand that we are not the sum total of our thoughts. When I carry around the equation DAVE = THOUGHTS, I become defensive. If people criticize what I think, then I feel that they're attacking me.

We can take this inquiry even further and look at our attachment to our emotions. Some people accept the equation I = MY EMOTIONS. So rather than experiencing the feeling of sadness, they *are* their sadness. Rather than feeling fear, they *are* their fear. They don't have emotions; their emotions have them.

I am not suggesting that people ignore their emotions. On the contrary, I think that the fastest way to be free of an emotion is to fully experience it. I am suggesting that we can have our emotions rather than allow our emotions to have us.

Although some people can accept the idea that they are not their possessions, their thoughts, or their feelings, they still carry around the equation I = MY BODY. This equation can lead to real upset during times of illness or impending death.

Just a few weeks before my father died, I called him to ask him how he was feeling. "Oh, I'm great," he said. My heart leapt, and I thought that perhaps he was recovering. So I asked him if the prednisone he was taking for lung cancer had opened up his breathing again. "No, no," he answered. "I can hardly breathe, and my body hurts. But I'm great." I then realized that my father had accepted his transition to death. He really knew that he was not his body.

If we are not our bodies, our thoughts, our emotions, our relationships, our possessions, or our jobs, then who are we? This is a question we can each answer for ourselves.

For me, the answer is that I am my conversations—the things I write about, read about, think about, listen to, watch, and say. Conversation cannot be taken away from me. Even if I lost my limbs or became paralyzed, I could carry on conversation. Even if I lost my speech, I could still be in conversation: I could write messages on slips of paper or point to a board that displays letters of the alphabet. I could listen fully and nod, shake my head, or blink my eyes to communicate.

With this view of who we are, we see that we transcend our physical bodies. Our conversations can continue long after our bodies are gone. When I return from a trip, I can still hear my mother asking about my travels and about what's new with each of my children. Even though she's died, I think about what I would tell her, and I can imagine her replies. In this way, my mother—that is, her conversation—is still alive.

With this perspective, we can stop identifying with our possessions, accomplishments, relationships, skills, opinions, expectations, and circumstances. When we see that we are more than our minds and bodies, we can feel secure enough to lighten up and let go. We can laugh hard even as we work hard. We can detach and play full out—a path to happiness that's available to us in each moment.

15. CHOOSE YOUR CONVERSATIONS
AND YOUR COMMUNITY

Right now you are awash in a sea of conversations. Your day might start with a conversation with your spouse or children about the fact that it's time to get up. Then you have conversations with coworkers, friends, neighbors, or relatives. There are also conversations with store clerks, bank tellers, teachers, supervisors, and many others.

To make sense of this strategy, expand your definition of the word *conversation*. This word can mean more than listening and talking to other people. It can also apply to the way we interact with books, magazines, movies, television programs, advertisements, and radio programs—any source of ideas or information. In each of these situations, we receive messages and respond to them. In each case, we're in a conversation.

Conversations can also include what we think—what we say to ourselves. These conversations take place inside our own heads and involve the constant stream of images and words that flow through our minds. Even though these conversations don't directly involve other people, they can be just as powerful as any other form of conversation.

Conversations can cross the bounds of time and space, life and death. We can watch films made by directors who are no longer alive. We can read books written centuries ago in foreign lands. We can listen to the lyrics of singers who have long since died. In some cases, the effect on us can be just as powerful as talking to these people face to face.

So, the first point about this strategy is that we human beings, always and everywhere, are participating in some form of conversation.

Here is the second point: Some conversations serve us well, and others don't.

Recall how it feels to eat lunch with a bunch of depressed people who complain all the time about how helpless they are. Afterward you probably won't feel empowered or enlivened, ready to sprint back to your job and do your most dazzling work. You might feel even more like settling into a blue funk, attacking a punching bag, or taking a nap.

Now think about other conversations that you've walked away from feeling energized, optimistic, and fueled for effective action. Compare those conversations to those that leave you feeling drained. There's a significant difference.

The same principle applies to the movies and television programs that we consume. Some of them ignite powerful conversations. Others leave us feeling dulled by irrelevance or dazed by violence.

Conversations have power. Our conversations mold our actions (what we do), which in turn mold our circumstances (what we have). This amazing dynamic is too often ignored. Most people let themselves drift haphazardly from one conversation to another as if they don't matter.

Instead of falling into conversations by accident, you can choose them. This process is especially powerful when you choose communities of people whose conversations steer you toward your goals and values. If you want to lose weight, you can start conversations with people who share that goal. If you want to begin exercising regularly, then you can start talking with people who have the same plan. You can even meet three times a week to talk while jogging together.

Sometimes taking charge of conversations calls for diplomacy. If conversations take a negative direction, you can switch the topic. If that doesn't work, you can ask directly to talk about something else. And if that still doesn't work, you can usually leave the conversation.

You can make a lasting contribution to yourself and to the people in your life by raising the quality of your choices about conversations.

16. REVISE YOUR HABITS

Imagine for a moment that the things we don't like about ourselves are just habits.

Our deepest emotional problems and our basic personality traits might all just be habits. A fit of depression that we blame on a childhood event—maybe that's just a habit. That roll of fat we blame on our lack of willpower—maybe that's just a habit. And that fit of rage we blamed on our hormones—maybe that's just a habit also. Stress, fear, rage, high debts, and other problems might be habits too—nothing less, nothing more.

Likewise, happiness, health, loving relationships, or wealth might be habits. The same could be true for personal qualities we admire so much—playfulness, forgiveness, attentive listening, and many more.

Maybe anything that we like or dislike about ourselves has a lot to do with our habits. Depression is one example. One possible source of depression is a biochemical problem that could be relieved with medication. Another source could be a bunch of small, unconscious habits. People who appear depressed often slump their shoulders, mumble, avoid eye contact, and move slowly and without purpose as they walk. Perhaps they spend hours mentally reliving a painful incident or plotting revenge on someone they resent. All these thoughts and behaviors are habits.

Optimistic and effective people display a constellation of habits, too. Often they stand erect, make eye contact, make animated gestures, and laugh. Their habits are entirely different from those of people who often feel depressed.

If all this is true, then solving problems and getting what you want in life might be as basic as learning to fasten your seat belt or to substitute herbal tea for coffee. Creating the life of your dreams could be as simple and as powerful as changing your habits.

There are many possible approaches to changing a habit. A simple three-step strategy follows:

1. *Commit yourself to change.* Publicly declare your intention to adopt a new behavior. Tell all the key people in your life about the change you plan to make. Put that change in writing. Make a formal contract with yourself. Then pledge to keep this promise with the same commitment that you would promise to repay a debt or tell the truth in court.

2. *Set up a feedback system.* Invent a way to see how well you're keeping your commitment. For example, you could create a chart with spaces for each day of the week, and then note how many times during the week you achieved the new habit. You could make a similar notation in your calendar. Or ask someone else to monitor your behavior and keep track of the results. If you want to change your posture, then ask people to give you feedback whenever they see you slouching in a chair. You could give your feedback system more teeth by building in rewards.

3. *Practice, practice, practice . . . without reproach.* Be gentle

with yourself. Habits often take years to develop, and they might not change overnight. It could take lots of practice. And remember that you can make mistakes without giving up on your commitment to change.

The beauty of this strategy is that there's no need to rummage around in the distant past, probe for causes, or blame those people and events who "made" us the way we are. Perhaps there's no need to judge ourselves for being failures. Instead of blaming and judging, we can just choose new behaviors. Taking charge of the future might be as simple as taking charge of our habits.

17. APPRECIATE MISTAKES

Failure is not fatal. Mistakes are no reason for misery. Goof-ups do not need to result in teeth-gnashing.

Our mistakes can be the most powerful teachers we have. What we learn from our mistakes is sometimes more instructive than what we learn from our successes—and often much more interesting.

If we truly realized the value of mistakes, we'd run the world much differently. We'd realize that mistakes are as important as successes. In addition to rewarding success, our society would recognize and even celebrate mistakes. Politicians might wage campaigns by claiming that they made more mistakes than their opponents did. Job applicants might submit "failure résumés"—highlights of their most fascinating goof-ups and what they learned from those experiences. (They could save tales of their biggest mistakes for the job interview.) Marketing executives might brag about the new products they pioneered that the public overwhelmingly rejected. And athletes might fondly recall the times they got trounced by opposing teams.

There's one sure way to avoid making mistakes, and that's to avoid doing anything. The writer who never finishes a book will never have to worry about getting negative reviews. The center fielder who sits out every game is safe from making any errors. And the comedian who never performs in front of an audience is sure to avoid telling jokes that fall flat.

We can find several reasons to appreciate mistakes. Mistakes have a way of focusing our attention and putting crucial problems right in our faces. Mistakes light a path for us. When we own up to our mistakes, we often know exactly what needs doing next.

Imagine working for a company where it is impossible to make a mistake. That could happen only at a place where mistakes were not distinguished from successes, a company that had no standards and held no one accountable for errors. Projects could go perpetually unfinished, and no one would say anything. Profit margins could fall through the floor, and no one would flinch.

In a situation marked by no distinction between failure and success, the word *mistake* would lack meaning. Mistakes can happen only when people are truly committed to making things work.

The greater our capacity to contribute to other people, the greater our potential for making critical mistakes. The chief executive of a corporation can make a decision that costs millions in lost revenue. The president of a country can make policy blunders that double the deficit. Even a highly trained surgeon can make an error during an operation that leads to the loss of life.

These same people can also be a force for good. A president can articulate a vision that unifies opposing political factions, executives can lead their companies into prosperity, and surgeons can save lives. In each case, people with the power to succeed also have the ability to fail. The two are woven together.

Benefiting from mistakes is not the same as setting out to make them. Learning from mistakes involves wisdom; setting out to make them involves willful incompetence. Effective people don't set goals with the idea of sabotaging their efforts. Rather, they aim to reach those goals while accepting the potential for error—and the potential for success.

18. THINK CLEARLY

You are always thinking. Whenever you reason, ponder, judge, believe, remember, imagine, plan, worry, learn, guess, or perform any other mental function, you are thinking.

When thinking is clear, organized, and logical, it often leads to useful distinctions and effective choices. When it is confused, random, and muddled, thinking can leave us with illogical conclusions and unwelcome results.

The ability to think clearly has little to do with IQ. Thinking clearly is a skill, a habit, that anyone can develop. What's more, this skill can greatly assist you as you create your future. Defining values, creating goals, and writing action plans are all exercises in thinking clearly.

Take time to be thoughtful

In the course of our daily lives, we are constantly confronted with issues and choices. Often, we habitually accept the first thought or conclusion that comes to mind. Doing this is easy, convenient, and seems to make perfect sense at the time.

But the first thought or choice that crosses our mind is not necessarily the most effective one. For example, many people who are searching for romance just go through life waiting, watching, and hoping that the right person will simply come along. An alternative is to be thoughtful. They could write down the personal qualities they want in a romantic partner. This document could help them assess the chances of having a wonderful relationship with someone they've just met. Taking time to think clearly about what they want could lead to a more healthy and enduring relationship.

One way to promote clear thinking is to speak about or write your thoughts, in order to organize and clarify them. Gaps in logic or mistaken assumptions then become more obvious.

Balance logic with emotions, intuition, and values

Thinking clearly includes balancing pure logic with our deepest emotions, trusted intuition, and strongly held values. Relying on logic alone is like trying to build a house with only a hammer. We handicap ourselves when we limit ourselves to using only one tool.

Let's say that you are considering investing in an exciting business with huge potential. Checking out resources, marketing plans, and income projections is crucial. Forgetting to consider these factors could cost you a lot of money.

In addition to relying on your logical business sense, you can pay attention to your emotions, listen to your intuition, and ask if this business is consistent with your values. If the bottom line adds up to fantastic profits but the product harms others or the environment, the cost to your peace of mind could outweigh the financial benefits.

Balance thinking independently with listening to others

A third guideline is to think independently while listening thoughtfully to others. Thinking independently prevents us from blindly adopting the ideas of others and caving in to peer pressure.

When we listen to the ideas and counsel of others, we can learn from their experience and wisdom. Balancing thinking for ourselves with listening to others gives us the best of both worlds.

Be careful of jumping to conclusions

Three common examples of jumping to conclusions are "either/or" thinking, generalizations, and exaggerations.

People who use either/or thinking might be looking for the security of certainty. It would be wonderful to know with certainty that things are either safe or unsafe, right or wrong, good or bad. If, for example, all members of one political party had high integrity and all members of the other were crooks, we would know how to vote every time. Unfortunately, few issues in life are this absolute. Flexible thinking allows us to explore a wider range of options.

Generalizations are tempting because they make life so convenient and predictable. If we jump to the conclusion that all people who have pierced ears and wear diamond earrings are thieves, we'd always be on alert when we're around them. Generalizations are suspect because they ignore individual differences. "All birds fly" is a generalization, and it is untrue. Penguins don't fly, and neither do ostriches. When you hear a generalization, be aware of possible exceptions. This could save you from errors in thinking and mistakes in behavior.

Exaggerations magnify things beyond truthful proportions. Some exaggerations are fairly harmless. When Bill talks about the fish that got away, everyone can roll their eyes and have a good laugh. Exaggerations can also be counterproductive, dangerous, or expensive: "You can make big money in multilevel marketing—everyone does." "Mutual funds are the best way to save for retirement." "Buying a house is a good investment." When you hear broad, sweeping statements like these, ask if there are possible exceptions—people who did not make money in multilevel marketing, other ways to save for retirement, or advantages to renting instead of buying. In these cases, thinking clearly can help you avoid errors in logic and protect your pocketbook.

Look for relevant arguments

Irrelevant arguments divert attention from the issue at hand. For example, a political candidate debating a tax reform issue accuses his opponent of failing to attend church regularly. A breakfast cereal company claims that its products are healthy because a professional athlete says that they taste good.

When listening to arguments, it pays to get past the fluff and uncover pertinent information.

Beware of false cause

We sometimes observe that one event follows another: Cold weather sets in, and then the car doesn't start. A friend gets fired and then starts drinking more. A student transfers to a private school and then gets better grades.

Be careful. The fact that two events are connected in time does not mean that one event *causes* the other. The fact that the car doesn't start could be due to a defective starter instead of the weather. The friend who got fired could have been an alcoholic well before he lost his job. The student who changes schools and gets better grades could also be getting more homework help from her parents.

One area in which cause-and-effect thinking can easily lead us astray is in explaining unwanted emotions. A person wakes up on a Monday morning feeling upset and concludes that her job is the cause. She changes her job and finds that she's still unhappy. So she goes into therapy and concludes that her unhappiness is caused by the fact that her parents divorced when she was a child. Then she begins searching for the cause of her parents' divorce.

A search for causes can lead to an endless spiral of explanations or even excuses—none of which lead to change. We can never be sure that an emotion has only one cause or that we've arrived at the "right" cause. In addition, this kind of searching often encourages us to blame others rather than take responsibility for the quality of our lives.

Often we can produce more happiness without focusing on all the reasons for our unhappiness. We benefit more from creating the future than from lamenting the past. Giving up the search for causes can free us to create the life of our dreams.

19. ACT COURAGEOUSLY

Courage is an old-fashioned word for an old-fashioned virtue. Traditionally, people have reserved that word for acts of the high and mighty—the campaigns of generals and the missions of heroes, the selfless acts of rescue workers during a disaster and the steely will of a mountain climber who scales the final dangerous cliff to reach the summit.

This concept of courage is fine. But it can rob us of seeing courage in everyday life. Ordinary people can exemplify tremendous courage in their daily adventures and struggles. Courage is the kindergartner whose heart is pounding with fear as she waves good-bye to her parents and boards the bus for her first day of school. Courage is the forty-year-old man who registers for college classes after twenty years away from the classroom. Courage is the woman who leaves her secure job with a public relations firm to work from her home as a freelance writer.

Each of us can search out examples of courage in ourselves and others. By noticing, talking about, and celebrating these everyday acts of courage, we increase the chance that courage will reoccur. When we heighten our awareness of courage, we begin to realize just how bravely we tackle each day of our lives.

Courage is not the absence of fear. Many people think that courage means feeling brave and fearless. When they feel fear before taking a risk, some people conclude that they're cowards. We gain a far more powerful perspective when we see courage as what we choose to *do,* even when we *feel* afraid.

Most people who ascend to the top ranks of their field feel fear. A famous actor can quake in his boots with stage fright before the curtain rises. A concert violinist can find her hands trembling before she sounds the first note of a concerto. A skilled teacher can dread the first day of school even after thirty years in the classroom. These people feel fear and choose to take action anyway.

If you comb through your personal history, you can probably recall many times when you acted independently of your fears. These times get to the essence of courage—you felt fear and still did what you intended to do.

Thinking about courage in this way reminds us that actions are much different from feelings. Whereas feelings elude our direct control, we can claim full responsibility for choosing our actions. We can feel depressed and still choose to do the laundry. We can feel homesick and still choose to do homework. We can feel lazy and still choose to mow the lawn.

Remarkably, you already possess this ability to act independently of feelings, including fear. There's nothing you have to do to gain courage—nothing you need to learn, no one you need to pay to teach you this skill. You can just use the skill you already have and apply it to more and more situations in your life.

Sometimes fear is a useful signal, and it is wise to choose actions that seem likely to reduce it. Walking around a lake rather than across thin ice is a good example of fear's leading to a wise decision. At other times, you might choose to do something that is likely to increase fear—for example, accepting an invitation to speak in front of a large group. That's a courageous and sensible act, especially if your goal is to give better presentations.

You can choose what to do, no matter how you feel. You don't have to be pushed around by a feeling. You don't have to let your emotions dictate your behaviors. You can fully experience your feelings, know all the details about them, and even celebrate them. And you don't have to obey them all the time. In any situation, no matter what you feel, you can take action consistent with your values and goals.

20. MANAGE YOUR ASSOCIATIONS

About twenty years ago, I discovered that within hours after eating sugary foods, I would feel sleepy. From my reading about nutrition, I learned that this is a common reaction. So I chose to stop eating sugar. But I wanted to make this lifestyle change with a minimum of suffering and self-denial.

Managing my associations allowed me to meet this goal. I just began looking at every bowl of ice cream and every piece of pie as a sleeping pill. Whenever I saw a dessert, I associated the taste of sugar with the feeling of being tired—a feeling that I did not want. As soon as I made this association, I found it easy to say no when someone offered me a piece of pie at a family dinner. I wasn't saying no to the great taste of pie; that would have required a lot of willpower. I was simply saying no to a sleeping pill.

Managing my associations also helped when my goal was to start exercising. Often I'd associated exercise with pain and discomfort. Then I started to see that when I exercised, I had a lot more energy throughout the day and thought more clearly. So I began to associate exercise with increased energy and clear thinking. Again, I was able to change my behavior with little to no willpower.

I share these stories to illustrate the benefit of managing your associations. When you want to change your behavior, simply change the associations that you link to the behavior. If you link a desired behavior to pleasure, you can begin doing it more often. If you link an unwanted behavior with pain, you can watch that behavior disappear.

The point is to consciously choose which behaviors we associate with pain and pleasure. Otherwise we live mechanically, merely reacting to external stimuli and random associations.

When we are unhappy, when our relationships are not working well, when we are not satisfied with our lives, it makes sense to pay attention to our associations. By learning to manage them, we can create new and more useful options.

When most people see a piece of chocolate cake, they associate it with the pleasant taste and the immediate stimulation they get from chocolate and sugar. Another option is to associate the chocolate cake with unwanted extra body fat.

To make this association more effective, play it up in your imagination. As you look at the cake, imagine that you can see past the attractive outward appearance of dark brown, rich choco-late into its core—a murky, yellow-brown mass of wiggly, layered, greasy fat. Imagine the putrid odor of the extra weight as it pre-pares to sag on the sides of your body. After thinking of chocolate cake in this way for just a few moments, it might require no willpower for you to say "No thanks."

We have a great deal of control over our associations, no mat-ter what life tosses our way. And the basic idea is unbelievably simple: Link what you want with what you already like. And link what you don't want to what you already don't like.

By making these links, you can approach living with more satisfaction and choice. What people perceive as steely-eyed willpower or superhuman motivation might be nothing more than your ability to manage associations.

21. CONTRIBUTE

Much of this book is about defining what our world would look like if we had everything we wanted. Most of the suggestions are about ways to have a more wonderful life—how we can achieve our goals and create the life of our dreams. Yet if we jeal-ously guard our happiness, we can become prisoners of our own joy. One way to get free is to contribute to the joy of others.

You'll probably find that once you achieve most of what you want for yourself, the next thing you'll want is to assist others to get what they want. This is the classic win/win philosophy. In giv-ing, we receive. In contributing to others, we contribute to our-selves.

One way to have the life of your dreams is to help other peo-ple have the life of their dreams. When people around you have more of what they want, you'll have more of what you want. If you want more love in your life, then assist others to have more love in their lives. Then, when you're surrounded by people who have more love in their lives, you will have more love in your life. If you want to be healthier, then find other people who want to be healthier and assist them. Form a support group to practice new strategies related to healthful nutrition, exercise, and stress management. This is one way help yourself become healthy. When you help others fulfill their goals, your goals ride along with them.

If you use this strategy, you could discover that contributing to others does more than help you get what you want. Contribution can also produce more joy than any of your other goals—buying a mansion, owning a limousine, or winning the lottery. Contribution is the last great hurrah, the ultimate Mount Everest to climb, the ultimate prize to gain. For many people—perhaps for all of us—the most lasting path to a life of ecstasy is contributing to others as well as to ourselves.

There are plenty of places to begin. At every moment, there are thousands of opportunities to contribute to the lives of others. You already know who could use your help—the children who die every day of starvation, the homeless people who sleep on the streets while inhaling car exhaust, the people addicted to alcohol who drink themselves to death, the teenagers slain by gang members, the people imprisoned without trials.

The purpose of bringing these facts to mind is not to depress you or to complain about how terrible the world is. Rather, the point is that you can begin making a difference. There is much to be done, and you can begin now.

As you take on bigger problems in the world, you could discover an unexpected benefit: Personal problems that used to seem so big start to shrink. Problems have a tendency to fill up the space that you allot to them. If the biggest problem you take on for the day is writing thank-you notes for a recent set of birth-day gifts, you could spend hours gathering the right paper and pen, deciding what to say, and driving to the post office to get just the right stamps. On the other hand, if, in the same day, you set a goal to write the thank-you notes *and* send letters to your repre-sentatives in Congress about the need for health care reform, you might be amazed at how quickly the thank-you notes get done.

By taking on a compelling project that extends beyond the concerns of your own life, you give your old problems less space in your life. Those old problems dwindle or even disappear.

In 1983, I was struggling with writing the third edition of a college textbook that wasn't selling so well. I noticed that when I got to work, I didn't want to write. I just wasn't motivated, even though I realized that, in order to survive, my new publishing and consulting business needed the new book.

I decided to test this theory of contribution. I got together with my staff, and we discussed what contribution project we could take on that would be worthy of our time and energy. We decided to end world hunger—no kidding. We took on the pro-ject of doing all that we could do to make a significant dent in the massive problem of thirty-five thousand children dying every day because they didn't have enough to eat.

We developed detailed action plans of what we could do as a group. These included educating ourselves, educating others, in-fluencing legislation, and contributing a lot of money to organi-zations that we thought were effective.

Writing the third edition of the book then became a means to an end—providing enough food for everybody on earth.

In the next few years, I incorporated education about world hunger into all of my workshops and my writing. And I was able to contribute hundreds of thousands of dollars to organizations that assisted people to end their own hunger. This approach produced not only motivation but also a wonderful sense of satisfaction.

While practicing contribution, some people become martyrs. They sacrifice their health and sanity in the quest to make life better for others. This could be called counter-contributing.

While working hard to solve big problems, you can also make it your goal to experience as much happiness, health, love, and wealth as possible. One of the most valuable gifts you can give to others is to be thrilled about your own life—a life filled with contribution. Through your happiness, you show people that celebration is just as important as problem solving. There may be nothing more contributive to others than your own ecstasy.

22. DEFINE YOUR VALUES AND ALIGN YOUR ACTIONS

Consider the importance of values. Values are our fundamental commitments, our highest principles, the things in life that we consider worthy for their own sake. Values influence and guide our choices. And our choices ultimately create the quality of our lives.

Some people have thoughtfully adopted a set of well-defined values. Others are guided by values that remain largely unconscious or unexamined.

Your values can be a clear, consistent guide to who you are and who you want to become. Investing time and energy to define your values and then aligning your actions with them is one of the most powerful ways that you can achieve the life of your dreams. Writing a clear and compelling list of your values can spur your creativity and suggest many worthwhile goals.

As you begin to define your values, consider those who have

gone before you. In creeds, scriptures, philosophies, hymns, myths, and sacred stories, the human race has left a vast and varied record of values. Be willing to look everywhere.

The following are some sample values, ones that I developed for myself. I created this list by going back to the values that I had heard of in Boy Scouts, in church, and from my parents at the dining-room table. I then spent hours talking to my friends and coworkers about what they valued. After coming up with my first draft of values, I then spent literally dozens of hours with an unabridged dictionary, looking up the definition of each word and the synonyms to which each definition referred me. After years of revision, I came up with these values—the ones I wanted to practice. And I revised them frequently.

I don't present these values here as the "right" ones for you. Please use them as just another reminder of what you want to incorporate in your own written value list.

Value: Be Accountable

This means being

* Honest
* Reliable
* Trustworthy
* Dependable
* Responsible

Being accountable includes making and keeping agreements —operating with integrity.

Value: Be Loving

This means being

* Affectionate
* Dedicated
* Devoted
* Equitable
* Accepting

Being loving includes appreciating myself and others—being gentle, considerate, forgiving, respectful, friendly, and courteous. It also includes being non-antagonistic, nonresistant, inclusive, understanding, compassionate, fair, and ethical.

Value: Be Self-Generating

This means being

* Responsible for myself
* The creator of my internal experiences—regardless of external circumstances

Being self-generating includes not being a victim and not blaming others. Instead, I choose how to interpret and respond to all stimuli.

Value: Be Promotive

This means being

* Nurturing
* Contributing—charitable, thrifty, and generous with time, money, and possessions
* Frugal—achieving the best results with the fewest possible dollars
* Helpful
* Encouraging
* Reasonable

* Judicious
* Cooperative—working as a member of a team or a community
* Appreciative

Value: Be Candid

This means being

* Honest
* Authentic
* Genuine
* Self-expressive
* Frank
* Outspoken
* Spontaneous
* Sincere
* Free of deceit
* Free of false modesty and arrogance
* Self-disclosing
* Open about strengths and weaknesses

Value: Be Detached

This means being

* Impartial
* Unbiased
* Experimental
* Satisfied
* Patient (not resigned)
* Open-minded
* Without distress
* Adaptable
* Trusting

* Tolerant
* Surrendering
* Joyful—fun-loving, humorous, lighthearted, and happy

Detachment includes being separate from, but aware of, thoughts, emotions, body, health, accomplishments, relationships, desires, commitments, possessions, values, opinions, roles, and expectations.

The opposite of detachment is being addicted (physically or emotionally), dogmatic, bigoted, absolutely certain, prejudiced, anxious, grave, or somber.

Value: Be Aware of the Possible

This means being

* Creative
* Imaginative
* Resourceful
* Inventive
* Capable of foresight
* Holistic
* Visionary
* Inquisitive
* Audacious
* Exploring

Being aware of the possible means expecting great things of myself and others.

Value: Be Involved

This means being

* Committed

* Participative
* Focused—precise and attentive to detail
* Enthusiastic—having intense or eager interest
* Enduring—persistent, persevering
* Courageous—vulnerable, willing to take risks, trusting
* Energetic—displaying capacity for action or accomplishment; being vigorous, robust, hardy, rugged, and strong
* Productive—operating with something at stake, pursuing excellence, acting with a sense of urgency without panic, and allowing projects to matter.

CHOOSE WAYS TO FULFILL YOUR GOALS

The twenty-two goal-fulfillment strategies outlined in this chapter can be applied to any of your goals. Before proceeding further with this book, write about ways to use these strategies to make a difference in your life.

Begin by listing one strategy in particular that appeals to you. Describe in writing exactly how you will use this strategy in meeting one or more of your goals.

You can return to this exercise many times to experiment with additional strategies. Consider writing about how well the strategies are working for you and how you can modify them to make them more useful.

Step 5:
Celebrate

*Change and growth take place when a person has
risked himself and dares to become involved with
experimenting with his own life.*

—Herbert Otto

*Let us put our minds together and see what life
we can make for our children.*

—Sitting Bull

KEEP YOUR PLAN ALIVE

Now that you've gone through the process of creating lots of possibilities, constructing a detailed plan, and carrying out part of your plan, I ask that you celebrate. You've done something very unusual in authoring your own life, and it's worth celebrating fully and completely.

And as you celebrate, I also ask that you continue creating your future. This chapter outlines many ways to keep your plan alive, to continue the planning process, and to bring this process to leaders at all levels of society. You can begin by experimenting with some of the following suggestions.

Stay in touch with your goals

You can start by staying in touch with your goals — literally. If you recorded your goals on 3 × 5 cards, then pick them up again. Reread those cards. Rewrite them. Sort them into new categories. Write new priorities, time lines, or partners on your cards. Even if you recorded your vision in a bound journal, computer program, or some format other than cards, you can still apply these suggestions.

You can use a variety of other methods to stay in touch with your goals. For example, if your goal is to buy a new car, then go to the dealer for a test drive. If your goal is to be debt-free, then ask someone to take a picture of you smiling and holding a bill marked *paid*. Do whatever it takes to physically contact your goals and keep your conversation space filled with the future.

Use frequent reminders

Take a tip from Madison Avenue. Advertising by spaced repetition of a message over time is worth billions of dollars to corporations. Imagine what repeatedly reminding yourself of your plan could be worth in terms of improving the quality of your own life.

Without reminders, even skilled planners can forget their goals. One solution is to post written goals in prominent locations—the bathroom, bedroom, hall mirror, or office door. Also, post goals on 3×5 cards and tape them to walls or put them on top of your bedroom dresser. Review the cards every night and every morning.

You can make your plan even more visible. Create an elaborate poster, sign, advertisement, or collage that displays your life purpose or lifeline. Use frames, color, graphics, and other visual devices to galvanize your attention. At one point, I covered a whole wall in my office with hundreds of pushpins where I hung thousands of completed 3×5 cards. You don't have to go to that extreme, but you could create a sizable picture, poster, or wall hanging that keeps your vision in front of your eyes.

You can also dedicate a special room or part of a room in your house to goal setting. Store all your planning-related materials in that location. Then, when you come to that spot, you'll get a subliminal message: "It's time to set goals and create your future!"

Be prepared to add goals

Goals have a way of coming to mind at the oddest moments—while you're waiting in line, riding the bus, or negotiating rush hour traffic. With a little advance planning, you can capture the ideas that pop into your mind at these times. One option is to carry a few 3×5 cards and a pen in your pocket or purse. As the advertisement said, "Don't leave home without them." Or pack a small tape recorder with you so you can say your goals and preserve them.

Enlist others to support your plan

Tell everyone in your life about what you plan to be, do, or have. Promise key people in your life that you'll achieve your high-priority goals, and ask them to assist you to keep these promises. Then if you ever feel like procrastinating or backsliding on a goal, you've got a reason to reconsider: "I've told so many people I'd do this . . . best to keep my word unless I'm certain that I want to change my plan." Making a public commitment can raise the stakes in creating your future and take the process to a whole new level.

You could even stage an event to announce your plan. One year before I finished the first detailed draft of my life plan, I publicly declared my intention to create that plan. When the draft was finished, I read it in the presence of coworkers, friends, family members, and a videotape recorder.

One obvious way to enlist the support of others is to ask for it directly. Explain how much the goals mean to you and what you'll do to achieve them. Mention that you're willing to alter the goal as circumstances change. In some cases, this might be all that's needed win over your loved ones.

Family members and close friends might balk at some of your goals: "You want to promote world peace. That's crazy! It will never happen. Why waste your time?" If you encounter such responses, remember that there are ways to work with resistance. It is possible to help your loved ones move from "Are you crazy?" to "How can I give you a hand?" One option is to *keep* talking about your vision and communicating how committed you are to it. Goals that sound outlandish to your family at first might become easier for them to accept over time.

Here again, you can take advantage of the power of spaced repetition. If you choose this technique, use it tastefully and with sensitivity. Repetition can become a counterproductive nuisance when it's overused.

Protect your goals from dream stealers

Dream stealers are people who discount your dreams or deflate your goals. Their tools are comments like these: "No one has ever done that." "Oh, come on, be realistic." "Just who do you think you are, anyway?"

Dream stealers could be anyone, even the most well-meaning people, even your spouse or best friends. These people might want you to be successful—but not too successful. Perhaps they fear not being part of your future. Or perhaps they fear that you'll be far happier than they ever hoped to be.

You can protect your dreams from dream stealers. Carefully choose the people with whom you share your goals. Begin by asking these people not to rain on your parade. Ask for their non-judgmental listening and enlist their active support.

Speaking about your goals with doubt or reluctance is like posting an "argue with me about this" sign on your forehead. To avoid this fate, release reluctance and give up shyness. Share your dreams with pride and enthusiasm. When you take this approach, others are more likely to respond in kind.

Seek out the dream catchers—people who are likely to support your goals and affirm your vision. Dream catchers might even see you as more loving, brilliant, and capable than you see yourself. With their confidence, you could expect your wildest goals to be easily achieved. Then you can start dreaming on an even larger scale.

Also practice being a dream catcher for others. Then when it's your turn to speak about the life of your dreams, they're more likely to return the favor and listen.

SHARE YOUR GOALS
WITH YOUR PARTNER

People can live together for years and have no clue about each other's desired future. This easily happens to people whose conversations center mainly on the past and present. The result is that we can fail to know something important about the person most dear to us—that person's vision of the future.

There is another option. You can regularly share your goals with your spouse or partner. You can speak in more detail about some of these goals, and that might lead you to create even more.

As you dare to share your future with your spouse or partner, you can learn new things about both of you. This activity can take an old relationship down new and exciting paths. You might even discover that some of your goals are the same as your partner's—that your chosen futures happen to coincide. What a joy!

Choose where and when you will share your goals with the key person in your life. Write some specific plans for doing this. Consider setting a date in your calendar for the sole purpose of revealing your future to the person you love.

KEEP THE PLANNING PROCESS ALIVE

At the beginning of this chapter, I wrote about keeping your plan alive as one way to celebrate and continue creating your future. It is just as important to keep the planning *process* alive. Continuing the process of planning allows you to constantly refresh your life plan with new and refined dreams and goals.

The suggestions described here can keep you in a conversation about the future for decades to come.

Create time to create your future

Talk about creating the future and you'll probably hear people say, "Yeah, that sounds like a great idea. I'll get around to that someday." Yet the long-awaited day might never come, and some people go to their graves without ever experiencing the benefits of setting long-range goals.

When you have a specific time to set goals and review them, you're much more likely to keep the process alive. Block out a regular planning time in your calendar. Make this an appointment with yourself, and treat it as seriously as a visit to your doctor.

Grab a few precious minutes here and there, whenever you can, to write goals. In sixty seconds or less you can jot down a goal or two. You can also set your wristwatch alarm for a certain time each day and give yourself five minutes to write goals. Think about goals while you exercise. If you walk, jog, or run with other people, you can take turns speaking your visions.

To keep the planning process alive, also create the time to reexamine and revise your goals. If you forget this step, your goals for the "future" might actually begin to represent your past, because that is when you created those goals—in the past. Acting on outdated goals could put you out of step with circumstances and keep you from creating the future that you really want.

Enlist partners in the process

If you want to get hooked on setting long-range, comprehensive goals, enlist some partners. Explain this process to your spouse, coworkers, children, family, and friends. Give them *Creating the Future* as a gift, and ask them to join you in long-range, comprehensive vision work. You could use exercises and readings from this book as a basis for your meetings. Remember that you can use this book many times—for example, once every year, every five years, or every ten years.

One of the rarest and most precious gifts you can give someone is the opportunity and encouragement to create the future. Set goals with people you love.

You can also enlist partners beyond your immediate family and friends. Read other books about setting and achieving goals. Listen to tapes and watch videos on these subjects. Attend workshops and seminars that relate to creating your future. You can use all these materials and events to stay in a positive conversation about the future and to affirm your dreams.

Find a coach

Perhaps a skilled planner would be willing to become your mentor. It pays to ask, and such a person might feel flattered if you do.

You can even hire a coach for goal setting—just as some people hire a personal trainer for help with nutrition or exercise. This person can assist you to set and meet long-range goals in all areas of your life. After giving and receiving this kind of coaching for over a decade, I find it essential to my effectiveness—and a big part of my joy in life. If necessary, I would live in a small mobile home or a one-bedroom apartment so that I could afford to hire a coach.

When you think, speak, and create goals in the presence of a skilled life coach, you can solve many problems without advice and without counseling. When you have regular support in the form of a coach's full attention, complete acceptance, and deep listening, you'll find that the answers to your questions are often within yourself. You can take the lid off your creativity. You're free to think what you've never thought before and to speak what you've never spoken before. In creating your future with a coach, you can uncover your genius.

Teach the process

There's a saying: We teach what we most need to learn. You can make this idea an incentive for creating the future. Explain this process to your friends and family members. Volunteer to lead a seminar, workshop, or community education class on this topic. If you have children, assist them in setting goals.

To help others get the most from creating the future, do more than teach—become a facilitator. Guide people through the process, perhaps starting with readings and exercises from this book. Ask them to speak often about their future, and listen with full attention to what they say.

Lighten up

If we're not careful, we can let goal setting turn into a chore or obligation. We can be far more effective by remembering to lighten up and have fun. Although creating the future can be serious, it does not have to become somber.

Creating the future can be an intense activity. It can also be a riot. Personally, I want to have a future with vibrant health, deep intimacy, daily ecstasy, and full celebration. One of my goals is to

have the *process* of creating my future take on those same qualities. I encourage you to also make creating your future a joy.

Monitor mind chatter

As you use the suggestions in this book, you might find certain ideas creeping into your stream of thoughts: "I'll never meet
any goal that's really important to me." "It's foolish of me to think
that I could ever have such a wonderful life." "Whenever I've allowed myself to dream, those dreams have always been crushed."
"People just don't change, and neither will I."

Thoughts like these put up huge obstacles to having the life
of our dreams. And those thoughts flourish when we keep them
inside ourselves.

Here's where we can use the power of writing and speaking to
other people. When talking to ourselves in monologue, we can
get a little crazy. But it's tough to stay crazy when we're talking to
other people. Dialogue shines a light on the beliefs that limit our
freedom. Once we bring self-limiting thoughts out in the open,
we rob them of their power, and we can find them far easier to
change.

Know the costs of creating your future

Most of this book is about the benefits of creating the future
and ways to make it a passionate, fun, and engaging adventure.
My own discovery is that creating the future carries costs as
well—sometimes big costs.

Perhaps you've experienced some of these costs already.
They can include upheaval of all varieties. You might discover
that you've been living without much reflection, unconsciously
repeating familiar patterns of behavior, or making choices based
on beliefs you no longer hold. You might become overwhelmed
by all the options that unfold before you and all the goals

you've promised. You might get in touch with regret over plans that fizzle or goals you fail to meet. You might choose to end long-standing relationships or take on a huge career change. Creating the future can introduce change that at first seems like chaos.

When you become the author of your future, you are—whether you like it or not—a leader. A participant in one of my workshops put it this way: "After changing my speaking so that more of it rests in the future, I find that others around me are speaking more powerfully. It's awesome to realize that I have the power to do that, and sometimes frightening." One mark of a leader is the ability to create and speak of a vision that moves other people into action. When you create the future, you might find that others request your leadership and raise their expectations of you.

Along with becoming a leader, you could feel isolated. Committing to create and live the life of your dreams is a wonderful—and unusual—thing to do. Leaders can feel lonely. Their capacity for vision sets them apart from the people who drift from day to day without goals or purpose, waiting to see what happens next.

Also, people might accuse you of being over-controlling, unspontaneous, egotistical, and uptight. There may even be moments when you wonder if they're right.

Creating the future could also uncover some habits that keep you from the life of your dreams. People report to me that creating the future highlights their tendencies to break agreements, to procrastinate, to blame others for their circumstances, or to give in to feelings of resignation. Discovering those habits is the first step to changing them, but making this kind of discovery is seldom easy, and it can even be terrifying.

Knowing and being prepared to deal with these costs can help keep your planning process alive.

Enjoy the rewards

The costs of creating the future are real—and so are the benefits. When we take on a project with huge risks, we often create the possibility of gaining huge rewards.

Taking the time to create goals and construct a comprehensive life plan makes it more likely that you'll actually have the future you desire. When crafting dreams and visions, you move from reaction to creation. Instead of passively responding to events, you start to shape them. Instead of complaining about circumstances, you get to create new ones. Those rewards are worth pursuing, even when they carry costs.

There are smaller pleasures as well. You can savor the feeling that comes with crossing items off your to-do list or moving your goal cards from the "to do" stack to the "done" stack. You might wish to save the cards filled with the goals you've completed so that you can celebrate your achievements. Or give those cards to others and suggest that they adopt one of your completed goals.

To stay in contact with these rewards, remember that creating the future is a choice, not a requirement—an option, not an obligation. My whole aim in this book is simply to help you shift more of your conversation space to the future. Once you've gotten a taste of creating the future and actually start living the life of your dreams, I trust that you'll embrace and enjoy this process for the rest of your life.

SCHEDULE A PERSONAL RETREAT

Make creating the future a useful habit by scheduling periodic breaks for rewriting your life purpose and setting goals.

You can turn these sessions into personal retreats. Take the time to take care of yourself. Write goals in a setting that you enjoy—in the woods, at a park, on the beach. During these sessions, take periodic breaks for rewarding activities, such as long walks at sunset or a massage. You can turn these sessions into opportunities for reflection, solitude, and quiet.

Please take the time right now to set the stage for your personal retreat. Write about where you will go and what you'd like to do on this retreat, and list some possible partners and dates for this activity.

START A CREATIVE COMMUNITY

Now, harness the power of community. Alcoholics Anonymous does. Weight Watchers does. So can goal setters.

When creating the future as part of a group, you can benefit from collective brilliance. Group members can coach you as you set goals and choose ways to fulfill them. That can be a real help on tough projects.

Your community can meet over lunch, after work, or via faxes, e-mail, conference calls—whatever it takes to stay in conversation about the future. You could even plan a multiday retreat. To get the most from your meetings, make them regular events. Meet at specified intervals—weekly, monthly, or quarterly.

No matter what activities you choose, practice confidentiality. Create an atmosphere of safety in the group.

Don't forget rewards. For example, you could stage an annual success banquet for your group. On that date, tell others about the goals you achieved during the year and those you plan to achieve next year. Also set aside time during the event for everyone to generate new goals and share them with the rest of the group.

Right now you could take the first steps to making this community a reality. List in writing the people you'd like to involve in your group and how you will contact them. Choose some possible times and places to stage your first meeting.

COMMIT YOURSELF TO THE PROCESS

Choose now what you will do to keep alive your process for creating the future. Review the list of suggestions, and choose one or more of them to actually use. Or invent other suggestions of your own.

No matter what you choose to do, turn it into a promise. You can begin by completing the following sentence in writing: "In order to celebrate and continue creating the future, I will . . ."

When you're done writing, sign this agreement with yourself and date it. Give a copy to a friend or family members who will gently remind you of your commitment and assist you to align your actions with your words.

LEAD YOUR LEADERS

Throughout this book, I have suggested ways for you to create hundreds of goals for yourself and the people closest to you. In addition, I have encouraged you to continue to create ambitious goals for your community, your city, your nation, and your world. My dream is that people in many nations will eventually join you in this practice of creating the future and that the result will be a comprehensive vision for all life on our planet.

Today we are in desperate need of such a vision. We can no longer assume that human society will progress, or even survive. Many forces threaten our species and our planet: nuclear war, dwindling natural resources, overpopulation, environmental pollution, deforestation, and more. Human beings might not thrive or even survive beyond the twenty-first century.

It's amazing that so many nations govern themselves with no coherent vision of the future. They pass laws, pursue policies, and spend trillions of dollars while leaving the future largely to accident. The blueprints for the survival of human civilization are vague or ignored, and immense costs flow from this fact.

A comprehensive, long-term, global vision could begin with ordinary citizens rather than with elected officials or think tanks that employ technical experts. The opportunity to begin and sustain a conversation about the future of civilization rests with you.

This statement is not an attempt to bash politicians or complain about the government. Many elected officials are honest and dedicated to public service. But every day these people struggle with forces that promote short-term thinking and narrow self-interest. Leaders are swayed by special-interest groups that lack a vision for the long-term future and the benefit of all beings. Television, newspapers, and radio stations are a means for public discussion, yet journalism seems to favor scandals and events of the recent past.

Since our leaders do not consider the long-term future, we can take the lead. While politicians come and go, we can begin and sustain a creative conversation about the future. What citizens can initiate, politicians can implement. We do not need to wait for others to take on this task.

By taking the time regularly to create the future, you can lead your leaders. It all starts as you plan, dream, invent, and set goals. Of course, I want you to create goals for yourself and start living the life of your dreams. This process can take on a new level of intensity and fun when you also state your dreams, visions, and goals for the future of our planet. You can merge personal and planetary concerns. You can think and act as if the future matters—for yourself and for everyone on Earth.

Bibliography

Bolles, Richard N. *The Three Boxes of Life and How to Get Out of Them: An Introduction to Life/Work Planning.* Berkeley, Calif: Ten Speed Press, 1978.

Covey, Stephen R., A. Roger Merrill, and Rebecca Merrill. *First Things First.* New York: Simon & Schuster, 1994.

Dominguez, Joe, and Vicki Robin. *Your Money or Your Life: Transforming Your Relationship with Money and Achieving Financial Independence.* New York: Viking, 1992.

Ellis, Dave, and Stan Lankowitz. *Human Being: A Manual for Happiness, Health, Love and Wealth.* Rapid City, S. Dak.: Breakthrough Enterprises, 1995.

Ellis, Dave, Stan Lankowitz, Ed Stupka, and Doug Toft. *Career Planning.* 2nd ed. Boston: Houghton Mifflin, 1997.

Frankl, Viktor. *Man's Search for Meaning.* New York: Simon & Schuster, 1970.

Gawain, Shakti. *Creative Visualization.* Mill Valley, Calif: Whatever, 1978.

Keyes, Ralph. *Timelock: How Life Got So Hectic and What You Can Do About It.* New York: HarperCollins, 1991.

Lakein, Alan. *How to Get Control of Your Time and Your Life.* New York: New American Library, 1974.

Reynolds, David K. *Constructive Living.* Honolulu: University of Hawaii Press, 1984.

Sher, Barbara, with Annie Gottlieb. *Wishcraft: How To Get What You Really Want.* New York: Ballantine, 1979.

Sinetar, Marsha. *Do What You Love, The Money Will Follow.* New York: Dell, 1987.

Winston, Stephanie. *Getting Organized.* New York: Warner, 1978.

Acknowledgments

Doug Toft is an amazing writer and editor. He has been wonderful at helping me express in writing what I generally present verbally. I thank him for being such a joyful coworker and future-oriented human being.

I also thank Stan Lankowitz who, for the past fifteen years, has been my dear friend, co-worker, and fellow author. This book exists largely due to his great ideas and constant support. Much of what is in this book was first articulated by him.

Larry David introduced me to the concept of long-range planning—creating the future—decades in advance. We started a business together in 1980, and when I was worried about next week's payroll, he was talking about his goals (limiting clients to those who would be around for at least five years, determining what philanthropic activities we would finance with our profits in the next twenty years, and persuading the United Nations to adopt a hundred-year plan for the governance of nations). I appreciate his opening up new possibilities for my life.

Thanks also to many people at Houghton Mifflin who worked on this book—particularly Marnie Patterson Cochran, my editor, and Wendy Strothman, the head of the Trade and Reference Division. They both saw the possibility of our creating the future.

I also acknowledge the wonderful support and partnership of my wife, Trisha Waldron, and my daughters, Snow, Berry, Sara, and Elizabeth.

Wanted: Your Ideas

Please help me write the next edition of this book. Sometimes, after a book has been written, rewritten, edited, designed, typeset, and printed, it is declared complete. That is not true for this book. *Creating Your Future* is still in development, and I will change it frequently as I learn more about what works for readers.

For this reason, I want to hear from you. Please write to the address below and let me know your reactions to this book. If an idea in this book doesn't work for you, let me know. If a technique is particularly effective, let me know that, too.

Thanks for your help.

Dave Ellis
13179 Baker Park Road
Rapid City, SD 57702

About the Author

Dave Ellis is the author of several books, including America's best-selling college textbook *Becoming a Master Student*, which has been translated into French and Spanish. This book is designed to promote student success inside and outside of the classroom. He is also the author or coauthor of the following: a book on career planning, a self-help book entitled *Human Being*, and a book that outlines a new career entitled *Life Coaching*.

Ellis is also a nationally known lecturer and workshop leader. He has facilitated four-day workshops on topics ranging from "Becoming a more effective college instructor" to "Creating individual life plans." These workshops have attracted more than ten thousand people.

Ellis taught computer programming at the college level and did accounting for an engineering research and development firm. He has also counseled college students, worked as an assistant dean of student services, and started and operated several businesses. In addition, Ellis founded a nonprofit foundation through which he has given away millions of dollars.

He has a bachelor's degree in psychology and a master's degree in computer science and has completed work toward a Ph.D. in psychology.

Dave is married, has four daughters, and lives in the Black Hills of South Dakota, where he writes and teaches at a retreat center that he designed.